BUCK & WART BACKCOUNTRY LETTERS

J. Wayne Fears
J. Craig Haney

Bannock Books

Copyright 2012 J. Wayne Fears & J. Craig Haney
All rights reserved.

INTRODUCTION

It was in the middle of the America's Great Depression. There was no money and most of the country's population was still rural and living somewhat off the land. Hunting, trapping, fishing, independent coal mining, digging ginseng and small farming were survival lifestyles necessary for the times. Many young men took to the rails trying to find work anywhere it was to be found. This was an era that tried America, but many backwoodsmen were up to the challenge and though poorly educated, with little personal property, carved out a life during these hard times, and enjoyed the experience.

This is a fictional collection of letters sent back and forth between two backcountry bachelors who grew up together in rural Alabama in the Cumberland Mountains. Buck Rivers stayed in the remote rural community of Tater Knob to live in his small cabin and to trap, dig "sang", farm a little and do small farm jobs to earn enough to not starve. Wart McGee had always wanted to experience life outside the mountains and valley around Tater Knob. When the Depression hit hard he just left one day, without notice to anyone, to try life on the rails as a hobo. After months of wandering, his luck changed when he won an Alaskan Roadhouse in a card game in Seattle. He went from Alabama hillbilly to Alaskan backcountry merchant with one good poker hand.

This is their story, and the lost story of many backcountry survivors of the Great Depression, told in a collection of letters. It is written as they would have written it. As was the case with many young rural men they had only an 8th grade education but what they lacked in polished English and "book learning" they more than made up for in woodsmanship and a lust for the outdoor life and adventure. This is their story, in their words.

DECEMBER 1931

Hello Buck,

It's me and I'm still alive! It's been quite a spell since I left the valley. I reckon I ain't seen ya since ol' man Garrett fell down drunk in the hog pen and suffocated in the mud. I'm just glad the hogs didn't eat him or mess him up so bad that the funeral home couldn't fix him up. He did have a right nice funeral though. Reverend Bates said some real nice things about him. Sorta made me wonder if'n he was talking about the same old coot that was lying dead and stiff in that pine box. I guess we think more kindly of folks after they're gone whether they're dead or just left town.

I never told you, but the wanderlust took holt of me just fore I left the Knob and wouldn't let go. I didn't want to bother anybody so I just up and left one morning fore anybody got up. It's been some ride. I run whiskey in Memphis, cowboyed in Wyoming, logged in Oregon and dealt cards in Seattle.

I tell ya what, I shore hated to leave Memphis, I was working at a bar-b-q joint called the Pork Palace. Their bar-b-q would eat good anywhere you took a bite. I mean it was good! But they made their real money selling white whiskey to the afterhours honky-tonks around town. I made a right smart a money just on tips delivering the shine but decided to move on after I heard Big Jack Quinn was coming in from the capital to clean up the town. That lawman has throwed more folks in the state pen outside Nashville than a skunk's got stink.

I rode the rails to Denver and on up to southeast Wyoming near Wheatland where I caught on at the Bar N ranch. Feller named Sam Neely run cows and horses on near 20,000 acres in the foothills and prairie. His foreman was a tough little Swede named Arnie Dubock. That man's tougher than a hanging judges' heart. He taught me to break horses and train 'em for cow duty. Those colts didn't wanna be rode no more than I wanted be throwed. I finally got my fill of it and headed northwest. Arnie'd been telling me 'bout his folks being loggers in Oregon and I decided that logging had to be easier on a body than breaking horses.

It took me a spell but I got up to Oregon in the logging country. I ain't ever seen trees so high or so green or so big around. Buck, they got saws so long it takes 2 men to use 'em and it still takes a bit of time to cut one of them trees down. That kinda work'll make a feller sleep real good. After working a full season, me and a fellow named Willie Bennett took the money we saved and headed for Seattle to see what a big city looked like. It weren't really no different than the towns we passed thru to get there, just bigger.

The saloons were a sight to see. They were bigger and more fancy than any I'd seen before, even back in Chattanooga or Memphis. They all got a piano player and a bunch of fancy women that dance on a stage in frilly dresses that don't cover up their good parts none too well. The card games played for a lot higher stakes than what I'm used to and the whiskey weren't as good as what's made back at the Knob. At my favorite joint, the Red Garter Saloon, Ol' Willie was using his money up pretty fast, 8 bits at a time, and I told him to slow down or he'd be broke with nothing to show for it but a big smile that's already done gone away. I'd been winnin' a fair amount at cards for a couple of days when I got myself in a high stakes game and it got down to a bruiser by the name of Israel Johnson and me left in it.

He was a sight to behold with thick, gnarly hair plumb down to his shoulders and a beard big enough fer a squirrel to nest in. He had 1 pigtail 'bout 6 inches long comin' off the right side of his head with some kind of beads painted red, yellow and orange in it. Said a Tlingit woman up in Alaska braided it and she said those beads kept away bad spirits. He said he guessed it worked cause he ain't been et by bears yet and ain't froze to death.

We'd been playin' 5 card stud fer awhile and when it got down to the final hand, that Johnson feller didn't have enough cash to cover my bet so he put up a deed to 10 acres and a roadhouse in Alaska to cover his bet. After we put our cards down, it seemed the luck done run out of those beads 'cause I won the hand, the cash and the roadhouse. I decided I'd head to Alaska to see what it looked like since I ain't never been there. With some of my winnings, I bought warm clothes for the cold country and booked passage on a steamer to see what my new property looked like. It was a cold slow trip up the coast on that steamer. Sorta missed ol'Willie on my trip up the coast, he'd been a good runnin' mate fer awhile and didn't like to cause no trouble.

I'm sitting here right now writing this in Wart's Roadhouse at Siler Pass. It's near Little Johnny Creek. It used to be called Johnson's Roadhouse but I decided to name it after me, Wart. We got nothing like this back home. It's part general store, part café, part hotel, part blacksmith shop, part post office, part feed store, part saloon, and all mine.

Been here about 6 months now but with all the snow, ice and wind, it seems more like 6 years. Lordy, I ain't never seen so much snow. I reckon when God ain't got no place else to put snow, he puts it right here. I'm sorta getting used to it, but then I ain't got much choice.

I got this young Cree injun gal, Lily Johns, that's as wide as she is tall and got hair as black as the blackest coal. She comes in and cleans up the private rooms as well as that nasty bunkroom upstairs over the feed section and the rest of the place also. I got 6 straw filled mattresses in the bunkroom, made of blue and white pillow ticking that I rent out to trappers, miners, hunters and other renegades that frequent these parts. She said them folks are nastier than any injun she's been with and smell worse than a ruttin' moose. She said the ticking is full of bed bugs and keeps asking if she can take home a jar of 'em to use for grayling bait. Now a grayling is sorta longer and skinnier than the bass and brim we got back home and they don't eat near as good. I'd give a pretty penny fer a plate of Mizz Blanton's fried brim and hushpuppies and some of them blackeyed peas fresh out of his garden. Oooowe!

Speakin' of them bedbugs, ya remember when we stayed in that abandoned sharecroppers' cabin back in the valley when we were makin' 50 cents a day splittin' locust for fence posts. Lord have mercy, it was hot! Must have been mite near 100 degrees and the humidity so thick it would have dulled that knife of yours if'n ya tried to cut through it. Don't know how them bedbugs could stand it, it 'bout made me loonier than ol' Billy Dale that lives up the holler. Anyways, you were gonna take some bedbugs home and try 'em for brim bait. Did you do it?

I laid in a load of firewood today and I'm right tired, so I guess I'll quit writin' fer now.

Yore friend,

Wart

JANUARY 1931

My friend Wart,

There have been bets placed at Miller's store that ye were dead or in prison somewhere. In fact Amos Trent and his wife were visiting relatives out in Indian Territory in Oklahoma and Amos swore he saw you working on a chain gang digging a canal or something. Then there was a rumor going round at the sawmill that you was working as a mule packer in the Swan Range country in Montana, packing with a fellow named Fenton Pardee. Anyhow, glad to hear from you and proud ye are a businessman now.
Be glad you're running a roadhouse and not trapping, farming or digging sang, this damn depression has got the prices of everything down to rock bottom. Last winter prime red fox pelts only brought $3.10 and I had to drive all the way to Huntland, Tennessee to get that. I picked up two road killed house cats on the last trip and sold them fer enough to pay my fuel fer ol' Lizzy. This year I have her up on blocks and I jest bought myself a black mule named Smokey. It cost a lot less to feed Smokey than to buy gas fer ol' Lizzy and I can use that mule fer farming.

By the way, I am renting that 10 acres down by Hurricane Creek where we used to shoot doves. I plan on planting cotton on it this spring. I trapped rats in the creek there all last winter and after looking at that bottomland soil, all spewed up during the winter freeze, I figured I could git at least a bale an acre off'n it.

You know that ol' Army surplus .30-40 Krag you sold my brother before ye disappeared? I borrowed it and a couple of shells and went across the Divide last spring up into the rocks at the top of Bice Mountain and hunted them wild goats that have been living there, free ranging, since those settlers moved in there after the War Tween the States. That rifle is sure one sweet shooting gun. I took a young billy at 175 yards with one shot. That were the easy part.

I dang near kilted myself gitting that stinking goat down out of them rocks, across the Divide and to Mud Spring where I could proper clean him. There was a couple of fellers putting up a sang digging camp at the top of Sneed Hollow and if'n it hadn't been fer them I would never got the goat there. It cost me a front shoulder, but well worth it fer the help.

We bar-b-q'ed the goat at Willy's gin and had a hoedown. The widow Sally Jensen came by in her fancy buggy pulled by that bay mare you always liked. She had some goat and a glass of buttermilk and asked around if'n anybody had heard from you. That's when Amos told the road gang story. She was shocked and promptly road off. I think she were embarrassed that she had once courted a man that was now a convict.

I trust this post will find ye well when you git it. I am leaving in bout an hour to run my longest trap line. It runs down Hurricane Creek to the Bales store then up the Waterfall Branch to the Waterfall then up to the top of the Knob along the high rocks there and then back to the north end of the Knob and down Skitter Creek to my cabin. I did all my sets fer coon and with a break in this dang cold weather I will be gone two, maybe three days, living on hoe cake and streak-o-lean.

Fore I quit writing, you ask about using them dad-blame bed bugs fer fish bait, Snake Larsen tried them one time fer brim on a size 16 hook and caught a few little ones. His biggest problem was they got out of the fruit jar he had then in and got into that old quilt he had in his fish camp and dang near ate him up one night. He said they bit harder than those at the sharecroppers' shack we stayed in that time. Let me know if'n that fat injun woman catches anything on em. If they work fer fish bait I could sell them to those city fellers that comes to the grist mill pond on Brier Fork Creek. They's always wanting to buy fiddle worms and such.

Next time tell me more about the country up thar.

Write when you can.

Buck

FEBRUARY 1931

Hello Buck,

I got so mad readin' your letter, I near 'bout swallowed my chaw. That Amos Trent can stir up more mess than anybody I seen. It ain't enough to spread rumors 'bout folk back home at Tater Knob, he has to go and do it while he's in injun territory. Truth told, I rode the rails so fast going thru Oklahoma, I didn't have no time to git in no trouble. I guess he's still ticked off cause I courted his wife back before he got hitched to her. I just couldn't get used to her having 1 brown and 1 green eye. She did cook a right good meal though and sure enough could make a good cobbler.

Sorry to hear fur prices are down, trapping is a hard enough job when prices are good. There a fair number of trappers up in this country. Here at the roadhouse, there's bout as much money tied up in trapping supplies as anything I reckon. Lots of different sizes of traps too. More 'n we use back home. Don't believe I'd want to get caught in one of them wolf traps. Them jaws are flat mean lookin' and would hold ya 'til Saint Peter called ya home.

Talking 'bout wolves, there's a trapper come by today with a sled full of what he said were prime wolf pelts. Said he was gonna leave 'em for the fur buyer that oughta be by in the next week or so. He was wearing a parka made of wolf pelts that he said a injun woman sewed for him and swapped him for some moose meat he had stored up in his cache. He was a right smart sized fella,' bout a half head taller than me and red hair and beard like you ain't never seen. Fact is, he come in the roadhouse with so much snow on that bright red beard it reminded me of them strawberry shortcakes your mama used to make back home with all that whipped cream. He's a Irishman. Onced he took off his parka and I could see his face good, he's got a real mean looking scar from near his left ear over towards his nose. I ain't bout to ask what happened. Maybe that scar is why he left Ireland.

He's a big brute of a fella with piercing blue eyes that could stare right through a chestnut log if he'd a mind to it. Said his name was Shamus O'Kelly and he'd been running traps out of his cabin bout half a days sled ride from here over near Porkypine Creek. He says he usually stays the night when he brings furs and gets what supplies he needs for his cabin. I got some caribou out of my cache and am making some stew with it. I added some potatoes and carrots and onions to it. It's smellin' right good.
Gonna make some sourdough rolls to sop up the gravy with but the starter that was left here ain't near as good as your aunt Lena's was. I guess you're still keepin' it going.

It's been right cold and with the wind blowing the way it does, it makes ya cold all way through ya innards. It was minus 31 when I checked the thermometer this morning. When I got the meat from the cache to make stew, I couldn't cut it with my butcher knife, it was froze so hard. Well, I finally figgered it out, got my woodsaw, and doggone if that didn't cut it. Made a little bit of meat sawdust on the ground and the birds came right to it before I walked away.

Before I got back inside, I noticed a fox skirtin' around the edge of the woods heading towards where I cut up the caribou meat. Ya reckon he smelt that meat from his den and decided to take a look. He was a pretty thing with that thick, bushy red fur and those black feet. That bushy tail was bout as big round as Granny Tomlinson's duster and had a bright white tip on it. That old hide buyer in Huntland, Tennessee would give a pretty penny for that pelt!

The woodstove in the middle of the roadhouse glows all the time this time of year. A feller will stay busy just keeping wood cut and stacked up for it, but ya gotta do it or freeze. Times it seems I cut wood half the day just to stay warm the other half. There's a bright copper tea kettle that stays on it most of the day with a steady stream of white steam coming out of its goose neck spout. Must be near new cause it ain't hardly tarnished none or dented up.

Anyways, 'cause of that kettle, I done started drinking a right smart of hot tea all day long to chase the chill away. Always thought the only menfolks that drunk hot tea were those Englishmen dressed in their tweedy clothes and wearin' them funny little hats. Doggone, I do miss sassafras tea and I believe mama could brew it up better anybody back at Tater Knob.

That injun, Lily Johns said she never did try them bedbugs for bait. She meant to but while tryin' to get 'em on the hook at Little Johnny Creek she kicked over the jar they was in and they went all over the place. Some run up her leg, some got in that coal black hair of hers and some fell in the creek and got eat by the grayling. I guess that means they was good fishbait.

I hope ya get the rain ya need for that cotton to grow like it oughta. That's a shore nuff good patch of land ya got but come pickin' time ya can't do it by yourself. Maybe ya can get some of the widow Duncan's kids to help ya pick it.

Lord knows with 9 of 'em she could stand getting some of 'em out of the house now that the older ones are big enough to help. Ya know cash money's got to be a mite short at their house what with her husbands' death and all.

Buck, I'd be much obliged if ya would tell Sally Jensen I weren't throwed in no jail or on no chain gang in Oklahoma. Ya tell Amos Trent I'm giving him a country boy butt whuppin' fer spreadin' them lies when I get back. By the way, how's ya brother and 'em?

War

MARCH 1931

Wart,

Yer letter came to my mail box while I was out pulling up my trap line. I spent two days down on the creek at Catfish Blanton's place cleaning traps and getting them ready to store fer the summer. I always like to do that work at his place as he is set up to boil traps and such down near the creek where he has his hog killin' set up. That scalding kettle will boil a lot of traps at one time. Plus his wife sets a good table. This time she served up some wood ducks with dressing that was as good as I ever ate. Catfish used the feathers from them ducks to tie some flies fer us to use later this spring. He said they would fool them smallmouths in the Paint Rock River and after looking at them I think he's right.

We had a shootin' at Willy's Cotton Gin last Saturday. I rode Smokey over there to buy some flour and such. I tied up in front of Miller's store just across the road from the gin and noticed that there was a number of the men in the community sitting around, out of the wind, on the sunny side of the gin.

They was a-whittlin' and I suppose they was talking bout turkey huntin' and the spring white sucker run. I threw up my hand at them and just as I got in the store I heard a shot, then several more. Sounded like popcorn a-goin' off. I turned around to see old Frank Johnson chasing Rob Smuller around a wagon hitched up to a team of mules. Now those mules weren't none too happy about what was a-going on. I thought they was bout to bolt and run over both Frank and Rob.

You remember Frank, always wore those blue bib overalls with the handle of that Owl's Head .38 always sticking out of that big pocket on the bib. Well, it seems that Frank was telling' about a big gobbler he had been seeing up in that beech tree grove behind the church and fore he finished telling' about the big bird, Rob jumped up and said it was his bird that he had been a-watching since Christmas. They said Frank got mad and started pulling out that Owl's Head and before he could get it out of the pocket, Rob pulled a little Colt .32 Auto out of his pocket and it went off just as it cleared his britches. It hit in the gravel at Franks' feet and when some of the flying gravel hit Franks leg, he thought he was hit and started chasing Rob, who was still recovering from the pistol going off, and chased him around Mr. Pickens wagon just-a shooting.

Men were ducking fer cover and bullets were a-flying all over the place. I looked at the commotion just in time to see Rob run under somebody's riding mule. It scared the mule and as Frank tried to go just behind that big ol' mule, it kicked Frank in the stomach.

Frank's pistol, now empty, went flying and bounced off the gin wall, then Frank went flying and landed in a fresh pile of horse apples. The gang at the gin started whooping and a-hollering and carrying on but soon they was all a-whittling and friends again. Frank had to sit aways downwind. Rob didn't say much about that gobbler the rest of the afternoon.

How do ye stand all that snow and ice? I saw a picture in one of them sporting magazines about trapping in Alaska and I do declare that is the coldest place I think I ever saw. How many pair of long johns do ye have to wear to stay warm?

Some days is warm here now, and I'm a-thinking about breaking up that 10 acres I rented down in the creek bottom. Like ye suggested I'm gonna talk to the Widow Duncan about getting some of her youngins to help me chop and pick cotton this year. The only reason I haven't gotten the place broken fore now is that with all the rain we've been gitting, the bottom is flooded most of the time and can't be worked. A few days ago on a cold morning, Catfish and I went down there and the whole bottom had a foot or more of water on it. We could see some big carp swimming around so we got down to our long drawers and waded in there with big sticks to try to club a mess of carp. Well, there was a deep little ditch a-running through the field that we both forgot about. We got after one big ol' carp and had him between us when we both stepped into that flooded ditch. It was neck deep and that water was as cold as anything I ever felt. The fish got away and me and Catfish had to run up on a ridge and build a fire fast. I don't think I have ever been that cold. Fresh carp jest ain't worth it!

I saw Sally Jensen at church Sunday and told her that ye weren't in no jail and was a businessman at Siler Pass. A smile came across her face like a wave on a slop bucket and she wanted to know more bout ye. Our conversation was a-going fine till I told her bout your injun woman and the bed bugs and suddenly she said goodbye. I think she still has a warm spot in her heart fer ye.

Well that's about it from the Knob fer now. I still got some fur to sell so I'm a-gonna hitch ol' Smokey up and ride up to Huntland tomorrow to see if I can make enough off my skins to buy cotton seed and such. I will post this letter at the post office there. Our mail carrier got drunk yesterday and ran his A-Model, wide open, through Widow Duncan's yard and killed three of her laying hens. The widow said they didn't need that much fresh chicken and she hit him over the head with a hoe handle and he had to go into town to get some stitches. I don't know when he will resume mail service here to our route.

Buck

APRIL 1931

Buck,

Doggone it, Buck, you 'bout screwed the goose when you told Sally Jensen about Lily Johns. Lily don't do nuthin' for me or to me but clean up around here. She ain't my injun woman. Your brain ain't no bigger than a blackeye pea that was picked too soon. Now ya go find Sally Jensen and tell her what's the truth. I don't want her thinkin' the wrong thing. Ya did say you thought she was still sweet on me didn't ya? Ain't saying I'm sweet on her but I don't want her mad at me if'n I get back to the Knob.

Other 'n finding out ya said something stupid to Sally, I'm glad to hear from ya. You made me plumb homesick talking bout it being almost planting time. Wish I could grow me some okra and turnip greens up here. I'd give a pretty penny for some fried okra, greens cooked with fatback and a big pone of cornbread. But here it is April and it's minus 2 degrees below zero and the ground is froze so hard that if'n I died, they'd have to put me up in the cache out back with the moose meat and caribou and wait 'til July to bury me. Leastways, I'm hoping this is the last morning I get up and see that red thermometer below zero.

You're right about Catfish Blanton's wife setting a mighty good table. I've had Miz Blanton's duck and dressin' once before. I reckon it was that November before the wanderlust took holt of me. I remember riding that bay mare of mine down to the Blanton's and thinking on the way that there can't be no prettier place than the Knob in November what with all them oaks and hickories looking like they been painted yellow and orange and red. She'd made up a bunch of fine eatin' fried apple pies from that tree over by the privy. You don't think that's why them apples grow so good, do ya?

Thinkin' bout all that good food back home has give me a stomach full of empty. All's I got is a pot of beans simmering on the stove with some moose side-meat in it. You remember back 'bout 4 year ago when we went over to Lacon Mountain to camp, fish Jig Creek and dig sang. You had that Colt Woodsman with you that you traded Billy Teague 2 prime shoats for. Remember, you got lucky with it and popped that crow that was sitting in that split hickory tree that lightnin' hit . You conjured up some right good stew with that crow, some dried beans and those wild onions we dug up. Wonder if'n one of them blasted ravens that are always hanging around my cache would eat that good if'n I stewed it. Probably not without some fatback to put in the stew.

Ther's a feller named Silas Wooten that brings up supplies ever month in a rickety old Ford truck that belches smoke, rattles and shimmies like a hoochy coochy dancer. I most always hear it a-ways out before it gets here. Well, he brought supplies in last week and spent the night as usual. I sawed off a big hunk of frozen moose hindquarter, cut it up into chunks with that Colclesser made Kephart knife I bought from that hardware store in Bryson City when we went up there to sell our furs. It's been a good knife, I skinned that cow moose with it and didn't have to touch it up. Use it all the time here in the roadhouse too. Anyways, that stew got to smellin' up the roadhouse so good, I couldn't hardly stand it. So I made me and Silas up some sourdough biskits from that recipe of yours. In all my my travels the last year or two, I still ain't ate any biskits better than yours made with that sourdough.

I'd picked a potful of gooseberries over near Little Johnny Creek just before the freeze and ain't done nothing with 'em so I decided to make us some gooseberry spread. I put the berries in a big black iron pot with a little water along with a generous dose of honey, a shot or 2 of corn syrup and a handful of sugar. When the pot started to bubble, I mashed up the berries with a wooden spoon I'd carved and kept a-stirring 'til it was just right. When it cooled, and it'll do it right quick when it's -5 degrees outside, I poured it into some canning jars I had and put in the pantry fer later. Now, I'm here to tell you it was some kind of good on them hot sourdough biskits.

Me and Silas was so full, we both turned in early. Silas went upstairs and bedded down in room 3. He usually sleeps in room 2 but I figger that last little bit of whiskey he drunk scrooched up his eyes so bad he couldn't see good and went into the wrong room. Well, 'bout 3 in the morning I heard a terrible goings on upstairs, there was screaming and yelling and first thing I know ol'Silas comes half running, half falling down the stairs. His face was as white as the snow outside and his eyes as big as hen eggs and he was just a-tremblin' inside those long johns.

He said he woke to use the slop bucket and there was a man in the room picking up his clothes and straightening the room. In a trembling voice, he said he could most nearly see through the man. He said he was dressed like a trapper excepting he was all clean and neat. I poured old Silas a stiff drink of rum and got him to calm down. I explained to him he'd seen the ghost of Dapper Jim Grimes who'd died in that room on his wedding night to a heart attack. The story goes that mail order bride of his plum wore him and his heart out that night. Don't know if'n it was true but she was 20 years younger, they say. It seems he comes back from time to time to find her and if'n he does , I hope his heart's a good bit stronger this time.

Well I got to quit writin' and finish my face mask I been workin' on. It's been so cold here at Siler Pass, I figgered my face was gonna freeze and fall off in chunks. After all winter, I finally figgered to take a piece of sheepskin big enough to cover my face, cut 2 slits for my eyes and tie it round my head with some rawhide string I made from that cow moose. Hope it will help!

Know it won't be long 'til the turkeys are gobblin' back home, let me know if'n ya kill one. Did that fly Catfish Blanton tied for ya from them duck feathers catch any smallmouth on the Paint Rock? I do believe them smallmouth back home eat better than the grayling up here.

It's gittin' late and I'm plumb tuckered out. I reckon I'm off to bed.

Wart

MAY 1931

Hello Wart,

Got yore post a few days ago and really enjoyed reading bout yore part of North America.

I ran into Sally Jensen at Mike Hollinsworth's funeral two weeks ago and got her to feeling good bout you. When we talked bout you she had a twinkle in her eye. So if'n ye get back this way I think you have an admirer.

You probably don't know bout it, but Mike Hollinsworth and a city dude was a-hunting goats up near the top of "The Walls" and Mike stepped on some slick rocks and his feet went out from under him and he fell off that limestone wall, near 150 feet straight down. He was still breathing when the city slicker got to him but the dude got lost trying to walk out and it was two days before he wandered into a farm near Skyline. When the sheriff got to Mike it was too late. I helped dig his grave, least I could do fer a good friend. They gave him a good sendoff. Folks thought a-lot of 'ol Mike.

Theys say that Mike and the slicker was huntin' that old calico colored billy me and you saw jest fore you moved off. You remember we saw 'em standing on a big rock on top of "The Walls" that day we was flyfishing fer redeye in that little creek that runs along the base of the cliff. Next winter I'm going to go back in there and hunt out that goat and pay him back fer Mike.

We had a hard freeze bout three weeks ago. It spit snow fer a day and fer three nights the ground froze and spewed up. The second morning of the freeze I was a-sitting in the sun behind my smokehouse whittling out some more mink stretchers when Catfish rode up on that one eyed horse he thinks so much of. Catfish had an idea that he wanted to talk over with me.

You remember that big flat field over at Doc Tipton's farm where we always shot so many doves, well Catfish had been thinking bout those hunts and how many quail we would see in that field after the dove shoots were over. He had cut open the crops of several of the quail he shot over there and found the quail were full of the seeds that the Doc had planted there fer quail. He ask the Doc what they were and Doc told him it was called brown top millet, a new plant from India.

Well, Catfish got to thinking and decided that if there were patches of browntop millet planted all over the valley we would have some coveys of quail that we would know bout where they lived. He got the Doc to give him a small sack of seed. Well, the morning Catfish rode over to my place he brought the sack of seed and we decided to ride all over the valley and everywhere we could find a bare spot of dirt that was frozen and spewed up we would sow some seed. We dang near froze to death riding and sowing but ye know what, I think that Catfish may be on to something. I look forward to going back to those patches later this summer to see if the seed come up and if the plants produce a lot of seed. If they do we will wear out that little English setter of Catfish's.

In ye last post ye mentioned that Kephart knife ye bought that time we was over at Bryson City. If'n you remember, I bought one of em Kephart Camp Tomahawks at that same hardware store. I keep that "hawk" in my hunting sack and it has come in handy countless times.

You mentioned that ghost you got in the roadhouse, it reminds me of the ghost we have over in the little graveyard up on the side of Lewis mountain. Have you seen that ghost yet that you bought with the roadhouse? You know haints ain't nothing to mess with.

So cold you have to wear a skin facemask in April? I'm glad that we don't have to wear face masks down here to get out in April. If'n it was that cold down here in April I don't think we would ever have a gobblin' turkey to hunt. Goodness, how do ye live where they ain't no wild turkeys? By the way I have bagged three Toms so far this spring. I have been a-using a little red cedar box call I made with a magnolia lid. It brings them ol' gobblers in a-running.

Tell me more bout yore country and what does that moose meat taste like? Gotta blow out the lamp and get some sleep. Tomorrow I got to work that bottomland I rented. If'n I keep writing you I will never get in a crop.

Buck

JUNE 1931

Hello Buck,

It was good to hear from from ya but it plumb saddened me about ol Mike Hollingsworth. You and me and him had us some good times growin' up back on Tater Knob. Skinny dippin' at the Green hole, coon huntin' with your Uncle Willy or sneaking off smoking rabbit tobacco, we always had us a good time. Hope ya nail that ol calico billy's hide on yore barn wall this fall.

As I write this, it's June 9 and the thermometer says 42 degrees. I bet it must be 85-90 degrees back home. All I know is I stay cold up here in this godawful country. I'm either a little cold, middlin' cold or a lot cold. It's purty country up here but I can't get the cold out of my bones. Maybe I'll get used to it, but I doubt it. By the time I drink enough whiskey to not feel cold, I don't feel nothing else either.

About the time I wuz getting lonesome for some company a few weeks ago, ol Red Dog Johnson come in with a pretty fair bundle of marten furs he'd trapped over the winter. I don't know much about them critters so over a supper of thick ram steaks, potatoes cooked in the coals of the fire and some dried pinto beans I cooked with fatback, onion and a little salt and pepper, Red Dog told me a little about martens. They're pretty smart little hunters and seem to favor snowshoe rabbits 'cause they're easy to catch and must taste good to'em. If it is a pore year for rabbits' they'll hunt squirrels, birds and mice, he says.

When the snow gits too deep to hunt mice on top of it, the marten will burrow in after the mouse and git him. I've found too that during the bitter cold winter, birds like the grouse and ptarmigan will burrow into the snow to keep from freezing. They won't burrow a little ways, no sir, they burrow a good ways down to git away from the bigger critters like foxes, wolves or lynx. That long deep burrow don't slow down a marten. He'll follow it all the way in and have him a good warm meal. Seems like the grouse and ptarmigan would catch on to the martens' tricks like they did with the foxes and wolves.

Red Dog said he puts out a fair number of deadfall traps to go along with the steel traps he puts out. He said he's got a favorite scent he uses made up of 1 part anise oil, 2 parts alcohol and 4 parts fish oil. He says its right fragrant and the martens seem to like it. For bait, he likes birds like partridges or the like and fish flesh is good too, he said. Trappin' up here ain't a lot different than what we do back home. Just different critters, sets and baits.

As May has warmed up, the woods are startin' to come to life a bit.. I wuz hangin' out my washing on the clothesline and some movement off to my right caught my eye. Seems it was a chickadee doing some spring cleaning of a knothole in a big old spruce. Now that little rascal was workin' hard bringing dead wood out of that knothole. I guess when it gits it cleaned out to its liking, it'll start building a nest inside and set up housekeeping.

The lake across the road is still froze over to my surprise but since this is my first spring in Alaska, I reckon I shouldn't let nothin' surprise me. Little Johnny Creek is the nearest creek to the roadhouse here that flows into the lake and it broke through the ice today. Maybe the ice on the lake will start breaking up now. When the ice is gone on the lake, I'm a-gonna put the canoe in and explore some across the lake.

I ain't seen that ghost yet but when Red Dog Johnson brought them furs in fer trade, he stayed over a couple of nights and slept in room 3 upstairs. When Red Dog came down the next morning, he had a right strange look on his face. I had a pot of coal black chicory coffee simmering on the stove, so I poured him a steaming hot mug of it and asked him what was wrong.

He said he knowd he'd leaned his .38-55 carbine in the corner of the room next to the bed and his clothes in a pile on the floor. Well sir, when he got up, the clothes were hung on the closet pole and the rifle was leaning against the chair. He said he knowd he didn't put 'em there. I told him about Dapper Jim Grimes dying while conjugatin' his wedding night with his bride. Folks say Dapper Jim's ghost stays in there waiting for his bride to come back. I guess he wants to keep the room tidy so when she comes back she'll be in a good mood and they can finish what they started.

Hope ya got yore crops put in and are getting a right smart a rain to grow 'em up good.

Gittin' tired and the candle's most burned down, so, I guess I'll stop writing.

Wart

JULY 1931

Wart,

I can't believe it was still cold in May. I bet ye wished you was still at your cabin on the Knob. It's near bout 100 degrees here on the porch according to my RC Cola thermometer. We need rain bad.

I got my garden planted and cleaned out the root celler. Had to get in it two weeks ago. I was getting ready to go fiddle me some fishing worms and was out at the barn getting my old handsaw that fiddles worms better than any other I ever saw. It was a-coming up a terrible thunder storm and on the way to the barn I looked towards the direction of Berry Mountain and here come a twister. It was kickin' up dirt, trees and somebody's tin roof. Well it looked like it was headed straight fer me so I high-tailed it into the root cellar with 'Ol Thunder and that 'ol black cat of mine right on my heels.

I heard it roaring like some kind of monster and it plum near blew the cellar door open. As we was riding out the storm 'Ol Thunder and the cat, both scared out of their wits, got into a fight over the back corner of the cellar and it was like a second storm in that hole with them going at one another. They broke two jars of tomatoes and a gallon of shine. The worst part was that they got hair and pee all over everything.

When the storm passed we came out and saw that the twister jumped up in the air over at Ned Bragg's place and went over my place doing no harm 'cept dropping somebody's ice box down near the barn. It's a good ice box and will make a good fish smoker if'n I don't find the rightful owner. I was lucky!

That storm taught me to never share a root cellar with a hound dog and a barn cat. I could of gotten scratched up bad. Come next storm they're on their own.

It was downright interesting to hear 'bout trapping martens. I've seen pictures of them in them outdoor magazines but I ain't never seed one to know it. If'n ye ever catch a few, send me a pelt. I will trade ye a prime rat hide fer it.

You was a-talking 'bout that ghost that lives in room number 3. Well that's like that ghost that lives around the old Cowart's graveyard at the foot of Lewis Mountain. That haint has been there some say since towards the end of the War Twix the States. They say it is the spirit of the boy they brung from a skirmish with the Yankees at the railroad crossing at Lim Rock. He was as dead as forge hammer when the .58 Caliber mini ball hit him in the head but some of his relatives loaded his body up in a wagon and bounced him all the way back here fer the burying. Well his spirit took offense to the long bumpy ride and ever since, he has raised Cain with anybody that come near the graveyard.

Old Doc Tipton hired me to go over there last summer to cut and split some cedar logs into rails fer a fence around his garden. Well, I set up a camp near the graveyard and commence to cutting cedar trees. When I returned to my canvas tent near the end of that first day, I saw my tent running down through the pasture. It was the first time I ever saw a tent a-running. When my mule saw the white tent a-running off, he lit out fer my place, leaving me on foot. I just knew it was that dead soldier's haint so I gathered up my gear and I skedaddled home fore dark. The next day Doc Tipton came by the house and had my tent in his truck. Fore I let him talk, I told him that that dead soldier's haint had run off with my tent and scared my mule plum near to death. Well the Doc got to laughing and couldn't talk fer near on to five minutes. "What's so blame funny about a haint stealing my tent", I asked him. " I seen it with my own eyes".

When he got where he could talk, he told me it weren't no haint. It seemed his old Jersey milk cow went in the tent to get to the peck of apples I had fer my lunches cause it loved apples and the fool cow got confused, and scared, and run off with my tent around it. Went straight to the Doc's place and into the barn.

Made me look like a dern fool.

I was down at the store the other day and ran into Sally Jensen. I knowed she was a-gonna ask bout you and sure enough she did. She shore is interested in you and I think she was trying to get up the courage to ask me to see yore letters. She wanted to know all bout yore road house and after Amos Trent telling her all that foolishness I had a hard time convincing her that an Alaskan roadhouse is not a honky-tonk or worse yet. When she found out it wasn't anything more than a trading post she seemed to be most happy. She said she had always thought about going to Alaska to visit one summer. Jest thought I would give you a warning.

She told me that there was a Winchester .32-20 rifle at her house that was yours. I thought it strange that you would leave a good rifle at a woman's house you was a-courtin'. I asked her did she want me to get it and keep it fer you. She looked at me with those devilish eyes and told me in no uncertain terms that you would be coming there when you came home and she would keep the rifle herself. I know there has to be more to that story but I ain't a-fixing to ask her.

I got my cotton and corn in, now we need rain. I got those injuns that live at the head of the creek to help me with the hoeing, coffee weed and morning glories worst I ever seen. Those injun boys are good workers and want to help me kill that man-killing calico goat that got Mike Hollinsworth. I'll be glad when cool weather gets here so we can go to the Walls after that critter.

Those browntop millet patches Catfish and me planted at Doc's when the ground spewed up this spring have come up and are loaded with seed. There is a covey of quail at each one. I can't wait 'til this quail season opens. I know where to find the birds. A mess of 'em fried up with some gravy and cathead biskits shore would be good.

Well I hear the chickens cuttin' up out back, must be a snake in the yard, so I will sign off on this post 'til next time.

Buck

AUGUST 1931

Hello Buck,

It was right good to hear from ya. You were plumb lucky that twister that come through didn't tear up yore place to speak of. They can be awful mean. I remember that one that came through over at Buggs Chapel a few years back. It picked up Johnny Rowe's homeplace and took it God only knows where. It didn't touch the barn or the hog lot. Woulda been a shame if'n it had took his hogs. Ol John always did make the best sausage in the county.

I couldn't believe it when he built another house smack dab on the same spot. Ol' John sure couldn't believe it when the next twister come through and took his house again. He and the missus got smart after that and moved to a place plum on the backside of Bice Mountain.

That gallon of shine that ol' Thunder and the cat broke, that wasn't some of that your cousin that lives over by Shelby Spring made, is it? That's some of the sweetest tastin' water I ever took a drink of. It shore does make good whiskey. Be a shame if a jug broke full of that Shelby Spring whiskey. Lordy, it would!

I know that story about the ghost at Cowart's graveyard must be true cause ever time I ever been by there, I got the goosebumps and the jibberwillies real bad. Haints ain't nothing you fool around with. I wish that one here at the roadhouse would git on out of here. I can't rent that room if'n a feller's heard of that ghost.

Sally Jensen. Sally Jensen. I'm shore glad she's still thinking of me. It'd tickle me plumb to tears if'n she did come up in the summer. I miss that smile and her way of lookin at me that gives me the tinglies. Course, I miss all the rest of her too. I know that when I think about her I get a heart full of empty.

Summer up here don't last near long enough. I got to start layin' in meat and supplies for the winter. There's a little repairin' I need to do to the roof of my cache and I'll git started on it onced I get this letter wrote. Shouldn't take me too long to repair it. Pesky squirrels chewed a hole in it wanting to set up housckeeping in there. I guess they figured it was a fit place to raise younguns. Well sir, thanks to that little Winchester Model 62 .22 pump of mine, they ended up in a pot with some mighty fine dumplings. They ate right good.

Last time that drummer Silas Wooten come through, I bought what's called a spottin' scope from him. It magnifies things 20 times closer to your eyeball. You screw it onto whats called a tripod to hold it up while you look through it. I figgered it'd be a help looking for sheep or caribou or moose when I was needin' to put up meat for the winter.

I took it with me when I decided to hunt for some sheep I'd spotted on Whiskey mountain not long ago. I loaded up my pack with some jerky, a little kettle, some tea, meat sacks, saw, rope and a blanket, put it in the canoe and paddled across the lake. After leaving my canoe tied up and turned over, I started walking in to Whiskey mountain.

After about an hour, I come to a good spot to set up that spottin' scope. And I did. I saw 5 sheep feedin' in a grassy area nearby a rock slide. That scope was worth the extra weight to haul it in. I figgered it'd take might near an hour to get myself in position for a good shot at one of them sheep. I set off and after a tough climb, come up behind a group of big boulders where I hunkered down. After catching my breath, I made sure there was a round in my 7x57 and slowly eased up to take my shot . Couldn't believe my eyes when I didn't see the sheep anywheres.

Then, I spotted 'em off to the left, held my breath and squeezed off a shot. That 7x57 did its' work, the sheep dropped like a rock. I hurried up to where it lay and got ready to dress it out. I got out my skinning knife, saw, meat sacks and got to work. Onced I got my packboard loaded with the sacks of meat I started down the mountain. It was a mite treacherous going down the mountain with the heavy load and took me longer than I figgered to get back to the canoe.

Onced I did, I set my load down and ate me some jerky with a leftover cathead biskit from breakfast and brewed me some strong tea. That food and tea gave me a needed boost and I loaded up the canoe. As I paddled back across the lake, I thought how good that tenderloin was gonna be fried up in my iron skillet with some gravy, rice and beans to go along with it. I wished I had put some dried apples in to soak before I left that morning so I coulda made me a cobbler.

I cut most of the meat into strips, seasoned 'em and put 'em in the smokehouse for a spell. I did save one roast and put it in my underground cooler box. This time of year, it stays 40 degrees inside the box even though its shirtsleeve weather during the day. I reckon later in the week I'll put the roast in the Dutch oven and let it cook all day with some onions and taters. Mighty good eatin', yessir, mighty good.

I've wrote about as long as my brain will let me for now so I guess I'll close. Tell Sally Jensen I sent my best to her and if she wanted to write I'd be most pleased.

Wart

SEPTEMBER 1931

Howdy Wart,

By grannies, that sheep meat does sound good. How does it size up to our wild goat meat? It'd have to be good to beat it.

Nights are a-getting cooler and there is a touch of fall in the air. I aim to go get that ol' billy what kilt Mike Hollinsworth so I am studying on how to come into the Walls from the backside. That country is so dad-blamed steep that old goat will never expect to see a hunter come in that away.

Thinking about that goat hunt, I got out that old war surplus Springfield Trap Door I have had so many years. I had a heck of a time finding .45-70 shells but the last time I went into town I went to the Montgomery Ward store and they's had them. Tickled me plum to death. That rifle will put that mean ol' goat down and we will have a bar-b-q at the gin in honor of Mike. That would have made him plumb proud. Soon as we get a killin' frost I am gonna go after that killer goat.

You mentioned John Rowe in yore last post. I rode ol'Smokey over Tater Knob to Bice Mountain last week to see if'n any of them settlers had sang roots ready to sell. Well, when I rode up into the Rowe's yard the misses came running out and was plum glad to see me, said I was the first outsider she'd seen in a month. She had a cobbler on the table and invited me in to sit a spell and eat some cobbler and have a glass of milk. I went in and saw that big old blackberry cobbler sitting on her table. I says to her, I says, "That's a-mighty fine looking blackberry cobbler ye have there." She looks at me kinda strange and waved her hand over the cobbler, well them blackberries all rose and flew around the ceiling. It was a peach cobbler! I ain't seen so many flies in one house in all my born days. It was hard to eat that cobbler knowing it had been a fly roost fer hours. But I had no choice. I grinned with ever bite.

Its been a dry summer on the mountain tops and ain't too many folks digging sang yet. They's say it will be a poor crop. Same fer golden seal. The huckleberries were scarce this summer also. Good summer fer cotton and it looks like I'm gonna get a bale to the acre on that bottomland I rented. If'n the price of coon fur don't get higher I'm gonna need that cotton money to make it through the winter.

That jug of corn squeezings that blamed Ol' Thunder and the cat busted during the twister was some of the best I've seen lately. That cross-eyed Morrison boy who lives down the creek near the church made the shine at his still that is in the head of Nance hollow. How it came about was, I planted a large patch of Hickory Cane corn last year to have some corn that would make good hominy. Well, Morrison heard about it and wanted to try to make some squeezings from it. I traded him a couple of bushels of the white corn and he gave me a gallon of the final product. Great stuff! I could have cried when it broke. This year I have three acres planted in Hickory Cane. I may make some hominy as well.

You mentioned you made dumplings. I have been making dumplings from that bannock mix recipe we use to use at our Soapstone Spring trapping camp. I know you must remember it – 1 cup flour, 1 teaspoon baking powder, ¼ teaspoon salt and enough real cold water to make it mix well into dough balls. Well take that and make small flat strips from it and drop in with ye boiling squirrels or rabbits. I jest wondered if that's how ye made your dumplings? Ye know we et a lot of that bannock back in those winters running our trap lines. Wish we'd made dumplings back then. We wuz a-missing out on some good eating and didn't know it.

You mentioned you had an iron skillet, glad ye have one. I almost sent you one bout two weeks ago and decided agin it fer it cost too much to send by post. Snake-eye Albright who has that little independent coal mine over on Coal Mine Mountain paid me good wages to take Ol' Smokey and to drag down to the mine some locust logs he had those injun boys of

Rose cut on top of the mountain. It was blazing hot and it took Ol' Smokey and me darn near two days to snake the logs down to the mine. After Albright paid me, I was a-walking Ol' Smokey off the mountain along the little creek that runs by all those abandoned mines. Well, we's going along when we came upon a sand bar. Instantly I spied something sticking out of the sand. It was the handle of an old cast iron skillet, rusty as all git-out but in good shape. I can't believe that a miner let a good skillet get away from him. Must have been when that flash flood of '24 wiped that mining camp out.

I took it home and sanded all the rust off'n it. That old skillet cleaned up real good. Knowing ye probably didn't have a good skillet, I coated it all over with some lard and set it over a little fire in my back yard. When it got hot, it soaked in that lard real good. Then I give it another good hot lard soaking. Turned out like a new skillet and is seasoned jest right. Since ye have one I will give this one to Sissy Stapler fer her dowry, she's a-getting married this fall.

Well there's a winter a-coming and I ain't split a stick of firewood so I will close and go to start my wood pile. I wish it were cool here like it is where you are, it would make splitting firewood easier.

Buck

OCTOBER 1931

Hello Buck,

You asked about does wild sheep eat as good as feral goat in yore last letter. If'n I had my druthers, sheep meat would be my choice. At least, wild sheep meat from up here. It's a sight better than farm raised sheep and a heap better than feral goat back home cause it ain't near as tough and stringy. Wild sheep's got a better flavor, too. I cooks it like I do steer meat back home. Just a little salt and pepper, ain't no need to try to fancy it up.

Now you let me know when you git that ol' goat what kilt our buddy Mike. I'll dance me a jig and toast ol' Mike with some of Tennessee's best whisky. That 45-70 of yours will knock that goats chin whiskers in the dirt fer sure. You be careful going into the Walls.

That's tough country up there. You'd best go down to Miller's store and tell Mister Arthur to git you some of that stout rope he sells to them loggers, something you know'll hold you if'n you fall from one of those high ledges. I don't want Sally writing me saying ya fell and got all broke up or worse, got yoreself kilt. But if'n ya did, I'd shore appreciate ya leavin' that little Kephart hawk to me. I'd think of ya ever time I used it.

An old sourdough drug in here the other day looking like death warmed over. He was all hunched over and could barely stand up straight. He stumbled thru the door with an old Winchester slung over his shoulder with a rawhide strap that looked like mice been chewing on it and 3 beaver tails tied around his waist. Said his name was Levi Proctor and he was a miner and just got in from a 3 day walk from his claim over in the Chilichatna Mountains near Minnie's Pass.

Said he'd found some color there but a griz had come in and wrecked his cabin so he thought he'd give that griz time to get done with it and he come back over to this area where he said he had a claim on the Little Fork of Horse Creek. It's 'bout a day and a half walk leadin' a mule loaded with supplies up there to Horse Creek from here at the roadhouse.

I mean he was a sight when he come in. He had a head full of white hair sticking out from under a black hat that was wore thru where he pinched the crown and what looked like a bullet hole about the size of a .44 in the brim. His face was ruddy and his right jaw was all swole up and I figgered he'd got a toothache on the trail and I was gonna hafta pull that bad tooth to relieve his pain and swellin'. But before I could say anything, he went over and spit a long, brown stream of tobakky juice in the fire. He turned around and that mop -sized white beard of his had a brown stream of that 'bakky juice coming down like snowmelt off the mountain. Right nasty lookin' if'n ya ask me.

He come over to one of the tables and sat hisself down and ordered a cup of hot, black coffee with a double shot of whiskey in it. That thick black chicory coffee was steamin' and when I pored that whisky in it, it smelt so good I got the thirsties for some myself. So I pored me some. After a second cup, he said his innards were startin' to thaw out and he was feelin' a touch better. He said reckoned he'd stay a couple of days at the roadhouse and enjoy some of life's pleasures like a hot bath and somebody elses cooking.

I put on a bunch more water to boil because he was sure nuff rank smellin' and it was gonna take a lot of hot water and lye soap to git the stink and dirt off him. He asked how I come by owning the roadhouse so I told him 'bout winning it in a card game in Seattle. He said the place looked better than it used to and got up to look and see what changes I'd made.

When he walked over to the mining supplies, I saw that raggedy, moth eaten old mackinaw of his had three rips down the back which made it kinda drafty for the upcoming weather which would be comin' in fore long.

I asked him about the tears in his coat and he said he'd left it hangin' on a peg at the cabin when he went off to work his claim. When he got back to his cabin, the coat was tore off the peg and a griz had done tore off the door and ransacked his cabin. Not knowin' when it might come back, he filled his pack basket quick as he could with enough supplies to git him here and took off a-hopin' the griz wouldn't come back and wind his trail.

Said he'd be lookin' for some new clothes onced he'd got that dirt and smell off. When I finally got enuff hot water for his bath, he went over and picked himself out some new long johns, tin pants and a moleskin shirt and headed for the room with the tub. Said he fancied some of those wool socks that Lily Johns knitted but didn't see none and asked if she was still around. I told him she was due to come in the next day or so from a trip she'd made to see some kin over near Magpie Lake.

When I told him she was comin' back, his eyes seemed to sparkle a touch and he got a slight grin behind that tobakky stained beard. Made me wonder whether he was wantin' socks to keep his feet warm or wantin' to git warm some other way.

Saw some moose sign when I went scoutin' for game the other day. I been cleaning my ol' Mauser 7x57 so it'll be ready to hunt cause I'm sure cravin' some fresh meat and I need to be putting some up for the winter ahead. Lily Johns wants me to get a moose so she can show me how to cook moose nose. She says its better than moose tongue, but I don't rightly know if I want to try either one.

I'll guess make some stew with the last of that sheep roast I got left over and have some beans and cornbread with it and make a pie with some fresh boysenberries I picked a couple a days ago.

Tell ever body back at the Knob ol' Wart says howdy. Yore pal,

Wart

NOVEMBER 1931

Lo' Wart,

Well it's time down here to start thinking about getting my trap lines set. I have boiled, died and waxed my traps and have scouted my lines. When I post this here letter I will leave to set my long lines around the Knob and into the Sinks. I do look forward to living on the trap line. What those city fellers miss, not huntin' and trappin' and such!

You really made me hungry writing about that ol' timer coming into ye store with beaver tails. I never et beaver tails fore last fall. I went over to the Snowbird Mountains buying sang and met up with an ol' trapper at the base of Granny Squirrel Mountain. That really was the name of that thar mountain. Well the ol' timer invited me to come spend the night at his camp and have supper with 'em. It seems that he had found a pocket of beaver way back in the mountains and was catching them right regular.

I told him we had caught out all the beaver where I live some 30 years ago and we didn't have any left. He said we's missing out on some good eating and the beaver fur were selling good.

That night he made a soup from one of them beaver tails and I tell you it was right fitten. I think it was better than the squirrel stew ye and me use to make when we had that camp in Hush Hollow. The beaver tail meat is white as snow and has a gelatin-like texture, strange to bite into, but sweet as a baby groundhog.

The next day I helped him run his lines and we took one of 'em ar tails and cooked it on an open fire fer lunch, man you talk about good, I wish beavers would come back here into Hurricane Creek.

You keep talking about moose nose but it's hard fer me to see how that can be fitten to eat. I guess it ain't too much different than a hog's snout. And that souse meat we make from a hog snout ain't too bad. Maybe if'n ye ever come home again ye can bring some moose nose fer me to try.

I guess the big news is Big Johnny, that injun kid that helps me around here a lot , and I took off to the Walls last week to look fer that calico colored billy goat that kilt Mike Hollinsworth last year. I took my .45-70 rifle and Big Johnny took his .32-40 Winchester 1894 rifle. We packed some bacon, bannock mix, jerky and beans on my packboard and Big Johnny had his pack basket in which we packed a skillet, coffee pot and a tarp. We each carried a new well rope in case we needed it to climb in that rockpile.

We got to the top of the Walls after a day of climbing, a coming in from the backside. Big Johnny got on a big timber rattler in the rocks on the way up and it made a fine supper. There are lots of wild goats up thar and it took us two days of slipping around fore we found that calico whiskered devil. I spotted him hidden at the base of a line of high limestone rocks near the top of Pitcher Ridge. It was like he knew we was a-huntin him and he was under a big rock in the shade, alert fer trouble. His horns were so big it was hard fer him to pull them in under the narrow rock opening.

Big Johnny and I made a plan and Johnny slipped south aways down the ridge and got on top of the ridge. I eased along a little creek and got below the billy where I could see him if'n he ran. I got next to a buckeye tree and waited. Big Johnny got on top and when he was about even with that killer goat he threw some rocks off'n the bluff. Just as soon as he did, that billy goat high-tailed it from under his hideout, straight down the ridge to me. I was awaiting and when he got about 50 yards away I stepped out from behind that tree and gave him a 300 grain bullet. It took the wind outta his sails and he fell dead, almost at my feet.

When Big Johnny got back down there we performed an injun ceremony to honor Mike and the calico billy goat. We hoped it would bring peace to both em ol' warriors.

We quartered the goat and saved the big curly horns. I had a place of honor I wanted to hang the big horns when I got back. It dang near killed me and Big Johnny getting all that meat and that big set of horns back to the road.

That Saturday we had a goat bar-b-q at the gin and everybody enjoyed it. I'am sure if Mike had been around he would have been plum tickled. It was kinda of a Mike Hollinsworth Day at Tater Knob.

Early the next day, at sunup, I took the goats' horns and rode over to the graveyard behind the church where Mike is buried and took a post and hung the big horns over Mike. I know it made him proud that I got the calico devil that got him. It made a right smart grave marker, if'n I do say so myself.

After church everybody went out back to the graveyard to Mike's grave to take a look. I know it's winter up where you are so I hope ye have plenty of stove wood cut, a cache full of meat, ye traps set and that ol' injun gal to keep you warm.

Jest as soon as I find an envelope to put this here post in I'm a-headed out to set my long lines. I hope to hear from you fore Christmas and I wish ye a merry one.

Buck

DECEMBER 1931

Hello Buck,

It sure made me proud to hear that you and that Johns kid kilt that old billy what caused Mike Hollingsworth's death. Huntin up at the "Walls" is a tough go and I know it was hard on you but you did the right thing to avenge Mike.

This morning, I got so gol-derned mad I could spit 10 penny nails. I went out to my cache to fetch me some fish for the sled dogs and a dad-blamed wolverine pert near destroyed everthing in it. It ruined my salmon, it ruined my moose meat, it tore up my extra snowshoes and got so excited it peed all over my boysenberries. Just weren't no sense in it! There's a good reason the injuns call 'em "Carcajou" or "Indian Devil" cause they're meaner than 18 Chinese rattlesnakes and got the Devil in 'em. They must be one part skunk, one part bear and all the rest is pure devil.

They're heavy critters, sorta bear-like in the way they look with big feet with white claws and a short bushy tail. They're colored real dark or blackish with a dirty yellow band that starts behind the shoulders and runs down each side of 'em and joins up at their butt. The back of their neck and head is a grizzled color. I guess some folks think they're colored up right handsome but they just look like trouble to me.

I'm glad they ain't real common around here. Least that's what Shamus O'Kelly told me this morning. Seems he come in from his cabin at Porkypine Creek for some supplies and heard me cussin and fussin out back at the cache. He says they'll eat anything from bugs to rats and mice to a bear carcass. If they find more food than they can eat at a sitting, they'll take some away and make their own cache. Now that's right smart of 'em. Shamus says they don't have no home territory but spend their time wandering, always lookin for new country. They don't den up like bears in the winter but will make a burrow under some deadfalls or other places where they feel safe.

Up the left fork of Porkypine Creek, winter two years ago, Shamus said one of them carcajou followed his trapline for miles and stole bait or tore up his catches making 'em worthless. Said he tried ever trapping trick he'd learned over the last twenty years to catch that devil but with no luck. If Shamus couldn't trap him, then I know they're tough to catch cause he's probably the best trapper in these parts.

Shamus helped me clean up the mess at the cache and get things pieced back together. I'm gonna have to get out in the next day or so to take another moose to replace the meat I lost. Shamus said he was gonna stay the night and could help me around the place if I needed him. With that scar from his left ear to his nose, he looks right menacing but he's got a good heart, it seems.

It's hard to believe it just turned December. The year has passed pretty quick, and there's been a lot to learn about running a roadhouse but I reckon I've learnt some of it. The cold has been tough to adjust to but I figger since I ain't froze to death, I'm doing pretty good in that department. There's enough folks coming by, trappers, travelers, hunters and homesteaders, that I don't get too lonesome but now that Christmas is a few weeks away, I'm starting to get the melancholy. Guess I'm missing family and friends back home at the Knob. Lily Johns made up some beaded pouches that she put in the store to sell. I bought one that I'm gonna send to Sally Jensen when Silas Wooten comes by with supplies and picks up the mail. I sure hope she'll like it and think of me when she looks at it. I can just see her now looking so pretty in that blue gingham dress with her blonde hair and sparkling blue eyes. That picture don't leave my mind too much and keeps me going at times.

I'm thinking about asking some of the regulars to come a day or two before Christmas and stay a couple of days here at the roadhouse and us have a Christmas get-together. I won't charge 'em for room and board. I thought we might all could use some company even though the trappers and the others that live up here are a solitary sort. I'll ask Shamus in the morning and see what he thinks.

I could decorate up the roadhouse for Christmas and cut me a tree to decorate and set it up across from the fireplace on the opposite side of the room. Don't have no real decorations but I can come up with something that'll work. I bet Lily Johns would help me even though she don't know about the baby Jesus and Christmas. I can explain it to her, I reckon.

Buck, if ya got time this winter, I'd be much obliged if ya would tie me up some flies like we use for smallmouth over on Paint Rock River. You remember the one don't ya? It's the one with the wood duck flank feathers for a tail, squirrel tail for a wing and that chenille yarn you got from your mama for a body. Use a middlin long hook about size 6 and I think they'd be just right. I've caught so many fish on it back home that I figger it'll be good for them trout and grayling what live up here. Ain't no big hurry, won't need 'em until May or June. If ya don't think ya can do it, then would ya mind asking Catfish Blanton for me?

I almost forgot to tell ya about supper tonight. On his way in to the roadhouse this morning, Shamus had a chance to pop a big ol' porkypine which he brought in for supper. After cleaning and skinning it, I cut it up into small pieces and boiled them with some salt and pepper for an hour or so. Then I added a cup of rice, 12 or 15 small dumplings I made from bannock dough and boiled it another 30 minutes or so in my big cast iron pot. I finished her up by adding a little flour to thicken the gravy. Hooee, that was some good eatin! I just wouln't have thought it from a porkypine. Ol' Shamus did good!

My lantern is about to burn out and I am too. Tell ever body back home Merry Christmas and I'll be a thinking about them. If ya see Sally, tell her I'm sending her a little something for Christmas.

Wart

JANUARY 1932

Hello Wart,

We all missed you during Christmas, especially that purty Sally. They had a Christmas pageant at the church with a big Christmas tree and fixings and the kids put on a Christmas play. Afterwards we had a dinner fitten fer a king. Due to this dad-blamed depression nobody had much money fer gifts and such but you stole the show, and from way up there! That Sally was showing off that fancy beaded pouch you sent her and all the ladies in the church were envious. I even thought I saw some of the men folk taking a second look at it. I have to admit it was right handsome and I would like to have that Lily Johns to make me up one to keep my .22 cartridges in. Is that tanned mouse rawhide or some other critter?

How was it to spend Christmas with a bunch of old sourdoughs? I bet you'll pulled the cork and ate some good vittles? We didn't have any snow but it were plenty cold. I guess you never have anything but a white Christmas up that way. You can have it. I don't need any of the white stuff here. It's hard enough making ends meet without all that shoveling snow and the mud that follows.

I got my fly tying vise set up on the kitchen table and I have a good supply of wood duck feathers so I will tie you up a mess of them Paint Rock bugs in a night or so. First I need to go out and see if I can get a new supply of squirrel tails. I am overdue for a squirrel stew anyway so I think tomorrow morning I will go over to that big oak and beech grove at Hush Hollow and see if'n I can't get a few. I will get you some of them Paint Rock bugs on their way soon.

Thinking of the Paint Rock River reminds me of the time you, Lard Miller and I went over there and fished the section near Princeton. We used some of them bugs, I think it were the first time you ever tied them, and caught a mess of bass. You remember 'ol Lard caught one of the bugs on a limb and when he were wading over to unhang it he slipped on a slick rock and went in over his head. It was the first real bath he had had in about six months. He looked like a hog trying to fly as he flailed the water trying to get out. You told him he left an oil slick downstream. I think you hurt his feelings. I miss those days. We had a lot of fun.

You mentioned eating a dad-blame porcupine and that it tasted good. I think your taste buds must have gotten hurt with all your traveling and such. From what I have read about one of them oversized pincushions I would think it would taste about like a coal oil soaked chittlin. Seems like a waste of good gravy to me.

Speaking of good vittles, ol' Catfish and I took that little English setter of his, you remember Kate, and went over to Doc Tipton's place and hunted those browntop millet patches we sowed last April. We got into a mess of quail. I bet there was one covey per patch and that Kate found three more coveys along that patch of woods near the old Jones place. I dang near ran out of shells. Well, Catfish and I took them birds over to his place and cleaned them. His missus took those birds and soaked them awhile in some muscadine wine she got from old Stump Gibson.

Then she seasoned them with some salt, pepper and powered sassafras, half covered them in some more of that wine and placed then in the oven to bake. While's they was a-baking slowly she made up a pot of black-eyed peas and some cathead biscuits. We ate like fatting hogs. She had fresh buttermilk to drink. Lord, were it good.

I ate too much and while I was a-riding Smokey home that night I dang near went to sleep and fell off. I was holding on to my sack of leftovers was all that kept me from hitting the ground.

I pulled my traps fer Christmas so now I am getting around to makein my rounds and reset them. Since fur prices are down with this depression and all it is hard to get excited about running long lines. I have been catching a lot of coons, possums and rats. It seems the fox and bobcat have moved out of this part of the country. Nobody in the valley or mountains are catching them. I met a smart young man over at the general store last week. He works fer one of them government game agencies. He was a-telling me that the shortage of fox and bobcat is due to the cottontail rabbits being in short supply the last couple of years. He told me that them rabbits run in seven year cycles with the numbers of rabbits either climbing or declining. When their numbers are low the fox and cat numbers are low. Makes sense to me. He said the cottontail numbers are starting to go back up and we will have good fox and cat trapping in a year or so.

You remember Toad Martin from down the creek, had that little place in the forks of the old wagon road near Brooks cave, well he was making some whiskey in the cave and his still blew up. The sheriff called it an explosion with a flash fire. It killed him and a black boy that was helping him. That was just fore Christmas. I was over at the gin when they rang the church bell to gather some men to dig the grave. I went over and it was so cold the ground was froze and all spewed up. Digging that grave was like chipping rock. We liked to never have gotten it deep enough to keep him safe. What was so ironic about the grave digging was that Billy Carter had some shine to keep us warm while digging and it was some of Toads finest. We had a little toast to him when his final resting place were dug.

Well that's it from Tater Knob. I got to get started packing to run my traplines and reset all them traps. It means several days of sleeping on the cold ground and eating hoecake and beans but you know Wart, I wouldn't trade it fer a new purty.

Fore I go I will tie up some of them bugs and get a package headed yore way.

See if'n you can get that injun gal to make me a beaded pouch fer my cartridges.

Buck

FEBRUARY 1932

Hello Buck,

Doggone you shore warmed this ol' heart talkin bout Christmas back home, particularly that part about Sally. I'm plumb tickled she liked that little pouch. That Christmas pageant at church will sure get you in the spirit what with the singing and decorations and all. And the food, ooowe, it's good. I reckon what I miss the most is them pies and cakes those 3 Tomlinson sisters would bake. Frances would bake a mincemeat, Sarah an apple and Elizabeth a peach pie. I never wanted to choose one kind over the other and hurt somebodies feelings so I'd get me a slice of each of 'em.

Christmas went right well here at the roadhouse. Four of the regulars came in on Christmas Eve day and stayed 'til the day after Christmas. There was Shamus O'Kelly, Red Dog Johnson, Sam McCord and Ev Turner. I cooked up a prime moose hind quarter with some potatoes, carrots and onions and it ate real good.

Sam defrosted some of my frozen blueberries and made a cobbler. It all musta been good, there weren't hardly any left. Ever body sorta pitched in while they was here. Shamus and Ev kept the firewood split and stacked on the porch. Red Dog kept the dishes washed up. Sam kept a harmonica in the right-hand pocketof a raggedy red and black plaid vest and ever now and again he'd play a tune on it. We all got sorta quiet when he played Silent Night. Maybe it reminded ever body of home and family and what might have been. I donno.

Over a breakfast of cathead biskits, sawmill gravy and moose sausage the morning after Christmas, Sam McCord got to talking about some caribou he had seen in a little valley on his way to the roadhouse Christmas eve. He said it was about an hour's hike from the roadhouse so we decided to go hunt 'em. After all, you can't never have too much meat put up in the winter. It was -4 degrees when I got up that morning but had warmed to +17 degrees by the time we took off to git us a caribou. I know your tryin' to figger out what a caribou is so I'll tell ya. They look like them reindeer what pulls Santy Claus's sleigh. I reckon they weigh around 3-400 pound and got a big conflagration of horns on top their head. They like to eat lichens. That's right, a big ol critter like that eatin little stuff like that but it makes 'em right tasty.

Walking over to the valley where Sam had spotted the caribou, it started snowing pretty good but by the time we got to the ridge overlooking the caribou, it had stopped. I hunkered down while Sam eased his way up to a big rock to make sure they was still there and feeding. He moved about as slow as those sourwood worms do back home in the spring. He finally got up enough to where he could see, looked for a couple of minutes through his 7x35 binoculars, then slowly eased down and come back to where I was. He said they was a mite far for my 7x57 and his model 1894 .38-40 and we'd have to crawl on our bellies a good ways to get where we'd have a shot. Crawling thru the snow didn't excite me none but thinking about some fresh meat hanging in my cache shore did.

We commenced to crawlin'. It was right hard on my knees. You'd thought that wearing long handles, wool britches and some thick wool overalls would have give me a little cushion on my knee bones but no. Anyways, we crawled from rock to rock to about 250 yards and then the sizable rocks sorta petered out for the next 150 yards and we didn't have much cover. But about 100 yards from the feeding caribou was a rock shaped like a 1-humped camel like was in the picture book back in school. Me and Sam got down on our bellies and started slitherin' like a copperhead in a blackberry patch. It was tough goin'. I was getting snow down my collar and sleeves and generally getting tore up by gravel, sticks and rocks.

Finally, we got to the rock and leaned back against it to catch our breath. Sam slowly eased up to make sure we hadn't spooked the critters atnd they were still there about 100 yards from us. If'n the wind hadn't been in our favor, they'd been long gone. They was pawin the snow to get to the lichens and slowly feeding broadside to us. There were 3 of 'em and about 15-20 more feeding further down the valley.

Anyway, we made sure our guns were ready and slowly eased up to where we could get a shot. We fired at the same time and it sounded almost like an explosion when them guns went off. Sam's went about 25 feet fore it dropped as dead as a hammer while mine only went about 7 steps and piled up. That little 7x57 done it again.

It didn't take long for us to get 'em gutted, cut the loins out and get the hindquarters loaded on our packboards. We covered up the rest of 'em with what sticks and grass we could find hoping to keep the wolves away. Maybe they wouldn't take to our scent around the carcasses. We knew we didn't have much daylight and had to get a move on. The snow had started coming down again but this time it was snowing mighty hard and made it harder to make our way. It probably took us an hour longer to get back to the roadhouse cause of the snow and all that weight we was carrying. Onced I smelled the woodsmoke from the roadhouse, I was a heap relieved.

As soon I opened the door, I smelt a fresh pot of coffee that was hangin over the fire. Ev had just put it on to make, a little while earlier. Lordy, Lordy, it tasted good and defrosted my innards and Sam's as well. We got the hindquarters skint and dressed out and put in the cache. Then I cut up the loin, floured it and fried it up and made gravy to go with it and boy howdy it was good. Red Dog, Shamus, Sam, Ev and me did ever thing but lick the skillet. Sam made some bannock with blueberries that made a right good deesert. I wished we had some of them caribou back at the Knob.

I was a bout to forget to tell ya that Lily Johns said she made them handy pouches from brain tanned beaver hide and she'd make ya up one to tote your 22 shells in.

Well, by the time ya get this letter, Buck, ya'll be pulling ya traps back there at the Knob, I reckon. Hope it's been a good season for ya. I'd be much obliged if'n ya tell me what ya caught and what kinda money they brung. I hope that Depression ain't hurt the prices too bad. I know one thing, good fur prices or bad, I shore miss running lines in that country.

Yore friend,

Wart

MARCH 1932

Wart,

Ye might be missing running those trap lines on the Knob but ye shore ain't missing nothing when it comes to making any cash from furs. This year the prices were at rock bottom and the critters seemed to have left the country. I think they know that there is a depression and they hightailed it to Mexico or somewhere. Plus this was one of the coldest winters we've seen in a long time. We had lots of snow and it made working my lines twice as hard as usual.

My long line produced 10 coons, 2 bobcats, 3 grey fox, 8 possums and 1 dark brown barn cat. I caught that cat way back on the fer side of the Divide. I wonder how a cat got that fer from houses. Anyway I skint the cat, trimmed the fur to look like a mink and sold him anyway. We had a dumb fur buyer that came by Bales store this winter.

My short line down along the creek weren't much better. I got 13 rats, 2 mink, 4 coons, and 1 otter. Between the two lines I didn't make enough to buy seed corn this year. This is gonna be a hard year if the price of cotton and corn don't go up. Somebody at the store last week said sang prices were going up this year so I might set up a camp near Callaway Sinks where you and I dug sang that hot summer in 28. There is a lot of sang in there and nobody has been digging there in the last couple of years. I miss our sang camps, it is a free life fer two ol' woods rats.

Dang if I don't wish fer some of them there caribou down here. They don't sound like they are too bright and that much good meat would do me fer a year. I wonder how Santa got those of his to pull a sled? Seriously, if ye get back down here I want you to jerk some of that moose and caribou meat. I dang sure want to try it.

Bean Hawkins was hauling some chestnut logs off the Knob last week and saw a herd of wild goats up on top of those cliffs on the north end of the Knob. I'm a-thinking bout heading up there tomorrow morning and see if I can get me a fat young goat to bar-b-q at the school fund raising. I suspect they are hanging out around that patch of grass near the Blow Hole where we caught that dark colored bobcat on New Years day bout three years ago. Bean said there was an ol' billy with a spotted coat of long hair leading the herd. He said its horns looked like they would run 36-inches. Now that's a trophy horn and would look good on Mike's grave. I just might try to get two goats. Those injun boys that live up at the head of Mountain Fork

Creek might want some fresh billy goat meat to make one of those injun stews they are so crazy about.

One chilly day last week I went down to the Tennessee River with Catfish to fish that big bank cutout that we use to shoot mallards in when you kept that flat bottomed plywood boat there. Well, our plan was to throw out a bunch of hand lines baited with fiddle worms to catch a mess of blue cats.

What brought this trip about was we had a warm spell a few days before and the worm fiddling over next to Hurricane Creek in that patch of woods on the Ray place produced a bucket of worms.

Well, we no sooner got those hand lines baited, and threw out into the deep pool in that cutout, when two fellows came walking up and joined us at our campfire. They were fishing down stream from us and heard us talking about fiddle worms. They wanted to see em. They had heard bout fiddling fer worms but didn't believe it to be a fact. Well you know how ol' Catfish can be when his methods are questioned, he jumped up and went to his truck and got out an old handsaw. With those two fishermen in tow, he went back in the woods a little ways and sawed down an oak sapling, bout 3-inches in diameter, leaving bout 16-inches of stump. He commenced to rub the saw on the stump so hard I could feel the ground vibrate where I stood. In a few minutes the leaves on the ground began to move and it was handfuls of earthworms coming to the surface. Catfish told the strangers that the worms thought the vibrations were moles coming to eat them and they skedaddled to the surface to escape.

The two strangers, turned out to be preachers from over near Gurley, left with a syrup bucket of worms and big grins on their faces. They told Catfish there would be a special blessing coming his way for sharing the fruits of the land. Lord knows he needs a special blessing poor as he is.

Once em preachers left we got back to trying to catch supper. The cold water gave the blue cats lockjaw, but Catfish, you know how ol" Catfish can be when it comes to fishing, wasn't about to go home empty handed.. Well he broke out his rod and reel and tied on a new jig he had tied at home one night. It was a lead head jig, number 6 hook, he had painted with a red head and a black eye. To the jig head he had tied a bunch of stiff white bristles. He called it a Do Jig. He tied it about a foot behind a silver Johnson spoon. He began to cast it around some tree tops that had fallen into the river during the winter. On his second cast he caught a slab size crappie. After that he dang near caught a large crappie with ever cast. I have never wished fer a rod and reel so much in my life as I did watching him. We left with a good mess of fish.

Speaking of fishing, I'm putting one of them Paint Rock Specials in this here envelope and hope it makes it up to you. You need to tie up a few and see how it works on them trout and grayling. Also I'm sticking in a few wood duck feathers and squirrel tail hair fer ye to use. If the bug don't make it all you all you have to do is to take a number 6 long shank hook and tie some wood duck flank fer a tail fer bout ½-inch. Then tie olive chennile at the tail and wrap it forward to the eye. Then tie some squirrel tail hair on it fer wings. I'm betting them yankee fish will take a shine to it. .

That's about it from th' Knob fer right now. I need to saddle Smokey and ride over to the Bales store and post this here letter if you gonna get it anytime soon. I'm still looking fer that beaded injun pouch to arrive.

Buck

APRIL 1932

Hello Buck,

I'm right sorry to hear that trappin' season was so doggone bad this winter. A lack of critters and poor pay for the pelts you do get makes a tough job tougher. Up here the trappers have done right well but like back home, the prices ain't no good. There seemed to be plenty of critters this season except for martens. Nobody did any good on martens and nobody could figure why.

Ya said ya had a bunch of snow that made running your traplines twiced as hard this winter. Don't know that ya would want to, but ya could come up here and run traplines next winter and ya could probably learn a lot about trapping in the snow that would help ya back home if'n it gets that bad again. Ya could stay here at the roadhouse and I wouldn't charge ya nothin'.

Settin' up camp at Callaway Sinks to dig sang just might help make up for the money ya didn't make running your lines this winter, particularly if'n the prices go up like folks think. I know ya gotta do something or you'll be broker than an outhouse rat. We did have a good haul of sang back in '28 at the Sinks and made us some money. I don't reckon I'll ever forget ya waking up that last mornin' with that copperhead snuggled up next to ya. Your eyes were big as saucers and ya looked like ya was tryin' to talk but no words were comin' out of your mouth. I'm just glad it decided to git on before I got over there to git it off of ya.

I'm much obliged to ya for sending that Paint Rock Special fly and the materials to tie it with. It's gittin' warmer up here in these parts. It was a high of plus 24 degrees today (Apr.2) and when the ice in the streams breaks up and goes away, I'm gonna try that fly for some of these trouts. If'n it'll catch them like it does smallmouth back home, I'll be a happy fella.

My stove ain't drawin' real good. I reckon I'll git up on the roof tomorrow and bang around on the stovepipe and try to knock some soot out of it. Maybe that'll help it draw better. Hope so, it's been gittin' a little smoky inside the place.

A couple of weeks ago, I gave Silas Wooten, the peddler, the pouch Lily Johns made for ya to mail when he got back to the post office. It was dadgum nice, made of brain tanned beaver skin, with a flap over the top that could be tied down. On the flap, she made a nice design with beads that she said would give you good luck. It's just the thing to keep ya .22 shells in. I don't know why I'm tellin' ya this, I guess ya got it already.

It's always nice to see ol' Silas here at the roadhouse. He's always got the supplies I need plus some new things to show me. He's about 5' 9' and sorta pudgy and always wearing a bright red wool scarf wrapped around his neck. The best thing about him is he's a right jovial sort and brightens up the place with his stories and jokes when he's here. We'll pull the cork on a jug and stay up late swappin' stories and tales. He's respectful of the jug and don't let it git the best of him which is good.

It was a right nice day today so I got out for awhile to see what signs of spring might be showing up. I guess I'm rushin' it but Lordy I'm ready for a change of weather, but warmer weather just don't come soon enough this time of year. Anyways, I got me some bannock and moose jerky, grabbed my rifle and headed out for a spell.

I stayed out most of the day taking in the sights. I seen some spruce grouse and the male was all puffed up showin' off. Bout noon, I stopped on the other side of the lake and built me a little fire and boiled some tea in my little kettle and ate my bannock and jerky. The kettle is black from woodsmoke and got more dents in it than my old liver pointer, Joe, had fleas. But it holds enough water for two cups of tea and comes in right handy on a day trip like this.

Heading back to the roadhouse, I saw a cow moose and yearling that was acting like they were in a hurry to git someplace else. I donno, maybe they caught scent of a wolf and decided to skedaddle. Later, I cut across some wolf tracks and I guess that was what had 'em spooked. When I crossed the creek near the roadhouse on my way back, I stopped and could hear water running under the ice. Now, that's a good sign.

You know, there is a lot not to like up here, bitter cold, snow, loneliness, but when I got out today and saw all the critters, it makes life more tolerable. It's big country, wild and beautiful in a special way. I guess God knew what he was doing' after all.

Enough for now, I'm plumb wore out after all my hiking today. Tell ever body (don't forget Sally) I miss 'em and hope they're doin' well.

Wart

MAY 1932

Howdy Wart,

I've been down in the bottom planting corn most of the day. I know it's late fer planting corn but this hard winter stayed late and has slowed down planting everything. It started to rain this afternoon so I brought ol' Smoky in, rubbed him down and decided to call it a day. The lightning is fierce and the thunder sounds like old Satan's shooting his cannon. Glad I ain't up in the mountains. I was up at The Walls one time back bout five year ago when it came up a storm such as this and the lightning struck all around me sending steam shooting up into the air out of them limestone rocks. My hair was standing up and I was jest bout as scared as a man can be.

Buckets full of water coming down on my tin roof right now, hard to hear myself think. Hurricane Creek will be running over it banks tomorrow if it keeps this up.

With this here storm going on, my house is dark as the inside of a black cat. I had to light the coal oil lamp just to see my writing paper.

I want to thank you kindly fer sending that beaded injun pouch fer my cartridges. It's too purty to haul around in the woods. I might tie it on my Sunday suit coat and show it off at church. Tell that Miss Lily Johns that I shore appreciate her going to the trouble to make it fer me. If,n beaver ever get back up in these creeks again I will trap me some and go into the business of making beaver pouches such as this. Them city folks in town would pay a purty penny fer em. But I doubt we will ever see beaver back up this way again. It's a shame that they were caught out back when their fur prices were so high. Dad-blamed people didn't have enough sense to leave some each year to replenish them what was caught. It were greed was what it was. You has to take care of wild critters jest like we do our livestock or one day there wont be any wild critters and I don't want to live where there ain't no wild critters.

They had the spring social at the church bout two weeks ago. Everybody brought a covered dish and I cooked goat and made up a big pot of hot sassafras tea. It were some of the best sassafras tea I ever made. The hard winter made the tree sap stay down in the roots longer so that when I dug the roots a few days fore the social they were full of sassafras sap.

Sally brung some of that fancy white china of hers, and you never seen so many country folks a-drinking hot tea with their little finger pointing straight up.

Looked like one on them fancy New York hotels at high tea hour. A feller new to the valley was there. Lem Pickens is his name. He is the new accountant over at the sawmill and he drives a fancy touring Buick. Well Lem talks like a city feller and dresses like one also. He has a lot to say bout worldly matters that don't make much sense to me. I think he has taken a shine to Sally and I heard him telling her bout how she should take a Sunday drive with him in his new car. She weren't interested but he is trying to get on her good side. Jest though ye would want to know. The ladies are saying that Sally is getting on to the age that if'n she's a-gonna get a man she better get on with it. Some are whispering bout her, calling her the spinster Jensen. Lord knows she'll pitch a fit if'n she hears that.

Ye know it's all yore fault, he, he.

We also had young goat on the pit fer the social. A week fore the big social, I took off early one morning and went to the top of the Knob. Ol' Thunder wanted to go, bad, but I didn't want no hound dog on a goat hunt so I tied him up at the barn. As I hiked up that mountain I could hear him back at my place howling his displeasure.

When I got to that cliff that circles the top of the Knob I climbed to the top, bout mid way between the north end and the south end. As I was climbing through the rock cliff I saw fresh goat sign everywhere. On top I caught my wind and started slipping north towards the grassy spot at the Blow Hole. I had my old Springfield, that I now call "Billy

Buster", after taking that ol' billy what got Hollingsworth kilt last year. Well as I slipped along that flat woods on top, the wind was blowing towards me from the Blow Hole and I smelled goats. I got behind a big chestnut and waited. Suddenly I heard the baaing of a goat. They were feeding my way in a big thick patch of tear britches greenbrier. Only a goat could walk through that stuff, and how they eat it I don't know.

Well I studied the little herd and saw the big ol' billy that Bean Hawkins saw, but this weren't no trophy hunt, I needed a fat nanny fer the church social. As I were peeking round that big ol' tree, that billy somehow saw me and let out a loud baaaaa and them goats hightailed it off that cliff as fast as I could get old "Billy Buster" up. One little nanny got tangled up in them greenbrier vines and was slow in making it to the edge and I nailed her. When she rolled, she rolled off that cliff and wedged bout half way down in some rocks. Now my hunt became a job!

I had to climb down in those rocks and, hanging on with my feet wedged in some rocks, field dress the goat. Then I had to get some well rope out of my huntin' pouch and lower that nanny down to the bottom. More than once I almost slipped off that spot. I thought, "Fresh meat fer the church social ain't worth dying fer".

I toted that goat all the way back down to my place thinking all the way what a mistake it were fer me not to have invited one of 'em injun boys to go with me on this hunt. They can tote a goat and not think nothing of it. It plum wore me out!

But once it was on the grill at the church and everybody bragging bout how good it tasted made it worth the while. We had some of that good vinegar sauce that I make up and that made it extra good.

Once I get layed by with my crops I want to take a trip over to Paint Rock River. Catfish tells me that the smallmouth over there are plentiful this year. Wish ye were here to go with me. The storms letting up so I gotta go feed my stock. Write when you can.

Buck

JUNE 1932

Hello Buck,

Ya sure know how to make a fella homesick talkin' about the spring social at the church. Next to Christmas, Thanksgiving, 4th of July, the Ramp Festival, the all day singin' with dinner on the grounds, the spring social is my favorite event of the year. Doggone it's fun and there's always good eats. I hope Tomcat Tomlinson don't win at horse shoes again. I don't mean it ugly but it seem's like he's won ever spring for the last ten years.

There's nothin' like pit cookin' a goat all night fer some good eatin', although I still prefer a slow cooked whole hog I believe. There ain't no such thing as bbq up here in Alaska and it's a shame. Now about that vinegar sauce of yours! Buck Rivers, you know and I know, and everbody at Tater Knob knows that I make a better sauce than you do and it's been proved ever time we have a bar-b-q back home. Folks always eat up more of my sauce than yours. You're still sore cause I won't tell ya that one secret ingredient that I use but you don't. Git over it Buck!

I ain't 'bout to git over what ya told me 'bout that city fella that's working at the sawmill now wantin'to court Sally Jensen. Ya need to tell him that Sally is spoken for and he needs to not be trying to court her. I'll tell ya something else to pass along to him. Ask him if he's ever had a country boy butt whuppin'. If he don't leave Sally alone, I'll flat leave this country and deliver that butt whuppin'. He'll be hurtin' all over more than anywhere else if he don't. By the way, ya need to tell them gossipy ol'hens that Sally ain't no spinster, she's waitin'fer the right man to come home to the Knob.

Whew! I sorta got riled up thinking 'bout all that. Had to quit writin', pull the cork on the jug and settle myself down some. Ya know how my temper is. I put on my parka and went outside for a few minutes to cool down. There's lights up here in the sky the locals call "northern lights." Anyways, they just go 'cross the sky in all kind of colors. It's really somethin' to see. Anyways, I calmed down and I'll git back to my writin' to ya.

When ya go over to the Paint Rock River, go down lower on it near the big river and fish that hole below the riffles at the corner of the Gardner place. If'n they wouldn't hit one of them Peckinpaw poppers what looks like a frog then I'd try that Paint Rock Special. There oughta be a good brown bass in that hole.

Ya know how I been waiting on warm weather. Well its' done got here and I'm plumb enjoyin' it.
Ev Turner was in the other day for supplies and to spend the night and he said he'd sleep anywhere other than the room where Dapper Jim Grimes died while conjugatin' his marriage. I said there ain't no such thing as ghosts but Shamus had told him back at Christmas about that room. We got it worked out, then he asked if I'd make up a batch of my sourdough biskits fer breakfast in the mornin' and cut some bacon off the slab and fry it up fer him. So I did and he ate like he was starvin' and then asked to take the leftovers with him when he left. He'd done that last time stayed, so I knew to make up some extras fer him. I don't believe he mixes his sourdough starter right with his flour when he makes biskits back at his cabin.

Ev said he'd spied a heap of cranberries growin' 'bout an hours hike from the roadhouse and he was gonna gather up some on his way back to his cabin. Guess he'll dry some fer later, maybe make some jelly and put some in some bannock. Anyways, I'm gonna go pick some tomorrow. It's never too early to lay in what you'll need fer the winter.

The ice is pretty much gone from the creek now. What's left is going downstream in chunks.The water looks sorta grayish right now. Lily Johns says it's runoff from that big blue glacier up north of here. She said it's so big it goes as far as yer eye can see. The stream should be cleared soon and it'll be ready to fish. Can't wait to catch and eat some fresh trout. The trout I canned fer winter ran out a while ago. It was pretty good but you know there ain't nothin'like fresh fish fried up with some onions and potatoes.

When I went over to the lake, the ice had moved out from around the bank and was breakin' up all across the surface. Ya could see the cracks ever where and the ice breakin' down into smaller pieces. Hopefully, it won't be too long before I'll be paddlin'the canoe across to git to my favorite fishing spot on the far bank near the pass between the two mountains. Speakin' of them mountains, it's mighty good to look up at 'em and see 'em sproutin' green from the new grasses comin' up on the slopes. The peaks are covered with snow but seein' that green grass always means it's a new beginning.

On my way home, I spotted a herd of 12-15 caribou 'bout 200 yards away. I got my binoculars from my pack basket and watched 'em awhile. They was grazin' along feeding on lichens when all of a sudden, they started actin' spooky and millin' around and finally took off. The wind was still blowin' in my face so I knowed they hadn't winded me. I figgered they musta smelt wolves or maybe a bear.

I didn't get back to the roadhouse 'til about an hour before sunset. Onced I got there I decided to make me some camp stew like Miss Elizabeth back home. She makes the best I ever ate. I didn't have chicken and ground beef like she makes it with so I substituted the last of my moose loin and I ground up a caribou roast. I peeled me some Irish potatoes and cut 'em into chunks about a half inch square and put 'em in my cast iron pot along with a big can of chicken stock. I put a handful of dried onion and some canned corn in too. Then I crushed some whole tomatoes in my hand and added them. I added some salt and pepper, covered the pot and hung over it the fireplace to cook.

I almost forgot to tell ya that I put in 4 or 5 shakes of "Wooster" sauce in the pot for flavor like Miss Elizabeth. It's what makes it good. That "Wooster" sauce is sure hard to get up here in this country. Silas finally had a bottle for me on his last trip. That's only the second bottle I been able to get in the year and a half I been up here. While I was waitin' for the stew to stew, I went outside and looked at the sun go down. It was a buttery gold color with some red and orange and was a real sight to see.

When the stew was ready, I fried up some hoecakes to go along with it. I fixed up a plate for me and Lily Johns and it was right good. The meat was real tender and the vegetables tasty though it weren't as good as Miss Elizabeths'. I ate me way too much and I'm startin' to get sleepy, so I guess I'll close this letter.

Hope your crops turn out good. Tell Sally I've sent her a letter.

Wart

PS: I almost forgot to tell ya Lily Johns brought me a cat. He's mostly grown, gray and didn't have a name so I call him Fred. He's helping to keep the ground squirrels out of the roadhouse and he's pure death on mice.

JULY 1932

Howdy Wart,

Be glad yore in the cold country up there. It's so hot down here that a fellow can't sleep at night and the snakes have plum disappeared. Yesterday I was over at the gin and some of the boys over there was cooking eggs in the sun on a piece of tin. I had heard bout that but never seen it with my own eyes.

The creeks are bout to go dry and the rivers are down mighty low. Catfish and I rode our mules over to Paint Rock River to the Garner place and tried that hole you was talking bout. The river was the lowest we ever saw it. We both took our fly rods and them dad-blame fish had the lockjaw until I tied on one of them there Paint Rock Specials. Well it was just one strike after another. We caught a mess of pan size bass and several slab sided bull bluegills. We cleaned em and took them over to Bud Hatcher's place and he cooked them up, with some fried sweet taters. I'm telling you that was some good eating.

The reason we rode the mules was that Bud had an old pole barn on the back of his place that was flat grown over with vines and such, so's that you couldn't hardly see it. Well he thought it was full of snakes so he wanted Catfish and I to pull it down and drag it where he could burn it. You remember how scared of snakes he is. That afternoon, after eating a belly full of fish and sweet taters, we went to that big thicket where the barn was and tied some ropes to the poles holding the old barn up. Bud was so scared that he weren't no help. Catfish gave him a hard time bout being scared of snakes and bout everything else.

Once we tied our well ropes to the old leaning shed, I gave ol' Smoky a loud "git up" and Catfish did the same for ol' One-eye and they dug in. The pole barn started fallin' in like there was an earthquake or somethin'. Bud was standing off to the side with his shotgun ready to kill all them snakes, when, as the barn started falling in, there was a loud scream, then another , then another and out of the viney rubble came several devil looking creatures, they's were a-running so fast that they looked liked various colored streaks, all headed straight fer where Bud was standing. Well, he screamed like a woman, pitched that old single barrel Stevens into the brush and ran into the woods faster than any man I ever saw run. Catfish and I 'bout hurt ourselves laughing. I never saw a grown man so scared.

All it was was a barn full of stray housecats. When that barn came down they had to run somewhere and Bud just happened to be standing there. For the past couple of years we've been wondering why there weren't no quail at Bud's, now we know.

When all that cat and Bud screaming commenced, it scared the mules and I had a hard time holding Smokey but One-eye broke loose and ran dragging a pole at the end of that rope plum to the river. Catfish made Bud go fetch him. It was a fun day.

Speaking of cats, where did Miss Lily get a cat fer your store? I would think that as cold as it gets up there the cat selection would be slim. Never knowed cats to like snow and freezing temperatures. Also, you better watch that cat when one of them trappers brings in a sled dog. Remember what happened when I put my cats and ol' Thunder down in the root cellar with me that time the twister came through? It could destroy your place.

You might of guessed it, that Tomcat won the horseshoe pitchen at the church again this spring. He even threw a perfect game, all ringers. Everybody was a-saying that no wonder he is so good as all he does at that job he has at the gin is pitch horseshoes. It is said that if ye ever come back home you might break his winning streak. You come closer to beating him than anybody else. Heck, you beat him at the ax throwing contest down at the sawmill and he has never shown up for it again. He needs a good licking at horseshoes as well.

The revival has been going on all week at the church. I bet it is over 100 degrees in that church each night and we have a visiting preacher from over near Buggs

Chapel that is a pure fire and brimstone preacher. He goes for over an hour each night and between the heat, all them wasps and a shortage of funeral home fans it makes for a long night, but he is a-saving souls. Why that mean old whiskey maker from over in Sutton Cove, Bark Taylor, went up to the alter two nights ago. Some say that his conscience is bothering him about selling that bad whiskey to them coon hunters two years ago. You know I don't believe that!

That sissy book keeper at the sawmill has been sitting in the same pew with Sally each night at the revival but she don't cut him much slack. She comes to church with Polly and Drew Perkins, and you know that Drew, he is protective of his sister-in-law and if that book keeper tries too hard Drew will clean his plow fer him.

I don't think that Sally has any man on her mind right now. I was told by that so called postman we have, Bill Askins, that Sally is bout to come into some big money and a lot of land from an old bachelor uncle she has out in Kansas. No one else in the valley seems to know bout it but Askins, but he swears it to be so. If I know that scroundel, he has been reading Sally's mail and everyone's else too. One of them injun boys told me he let the store up at Huntland keep his bobcat pelts on consignment last winter until the fur buyer came through. Well they got a good price fer them and sent the injun a check in the mail. Before that injun had time to open his envelope, Askins had told the boys at the gin how much he got. That boy told me that the next time that happened we would be a-needing a postman and you know how those injun boys are, they don't just say something to hear how it sounds.

Anyway Sally may be about to change her financial status.

Well I got to get ol' Thunder and go look fer that milk cow of mine. She is with calf, no thanks to Catfish's wormy bull getting out last winter, and she didn't come to the barn tonight. When she has a calf she can get as mean as a cornered groundhog. I think she is up in that big stand of beech trees near my bee gums so that means I have a bit of walking to do.

Write when ye can and send some of that cool weather. I'm 'bout to burn up sitting at this lamp writing.

Buck

AUGUST 1932

Hello Buck,

Ya gone and done it again talkin' 'bout food back home. Now ya got me cravin' some bluegill and bass all fried up crispy with sweet potato fries , vinegar slaw and Katie Sue's hushpuppies. Ol' Bud Hatcher did himself proud when he married that gal! She can flat cook and she's a looker, too. Ya can't beat that combination, I do believe.

I wished I coulda seen Bud take off running and a screamin' when them devil cats tore outta the barn. I know he's plum embarrassed 'bout it now and probably worried yore gonna tell the fellas down at the gin 'bout how he took off screamin' like a woman.

Ya asked 'bout the cat Lily Johns give me fer the roadhouse. Well sir, I asked how she come by that cat and she said she got it from her cousin who'd come to visit. He lives over in the Yukon Territory and brought her 3 kittens when he come to visit last time.

Said he'd got 'em from one of the Mounties at the Royal Canadian Mounted Police station about ½ mile from his cabin. He said he brought three 'cause he figgered one would die of the blasted cold, one would git eat by a critter and that'd leave her 1 to keep in her cabin to keep the place rid of mice and them pesky ground squirrels.

Ya say Tomcat won the horseshoe championship again, did ya. After hearing about that, I ordered me up a set of horseshoes from Montgomery Ward and figgered I'd just start practicin' so when I git home I'll be ready to take him on. The day they finally come in, Shamus was here gittin' supplied up fer the next few weeks and saw me open up the box and take 'em out. I laid ever thing out on the bar and he stared at the horseshoes with those piercin' blue eyes of his, then looked at me and said there ain't a horse back home in County Cork big enough to wear them horse shoes. Besides, he said, what kinda fool would paint good horseshoes red or yeller? I said they was painted so when ya throwed 'em, ya could tell 'em apart when they landed. Then he asked why a fella would throw 'em to start with?

Red Dog Johnson and Ev Turner came by the place a couple of days later and saw where I'd set up the horseshoe pit out back by the cache. Ev got to jawin' about how nobody could beat him back home in northern South Dakota where he came from and he challenged me to a game. We got to throwin' the horseshoes and I let him win 3 out of 4 games. "Bout that time, Red Dog said why don't you boys put a little wager on it to make it more interesting. Buck, that was music to my ears. Ev jumped on it like a brim on a catalpa worm and I played hard to get. Finally, I let Ev talk me into it. It was hard to keep from grinnin'! By the time we got through, I'd won all his cash (weren't much), that bone handled XX Case knife of his and a prime lynx pelt along with a couple of marten pelts. I reckon I should have felt bad but I didn't 'cause Ev let his mouth overload his fanny after I let him win the first couple of games.

I'm glad fer Sally that she might come into some money from that uncle of hers. We were cuttin' a watermelon over at Hurricane Creek, near where that little feeder creek comes in by the Sivley place, a couple of year ago and she started talkin' 'bout her family. He's her uncle on her mother's side of the family. They hail from over around Decatur. He didn't take to farming like her daddy and Grandpa. He went off to Florence State Teachers College to git an education and ended up becoming a banker. I believe his name was William Augustus Randolph. That sounds like a banker's name, don't it? Her daddy told her it most nearly killed their Pa who didn't trust bankers. The old man said he'd rather him been a bank robber that a banker. It was a more honorable job, at least ya knew what their intent was.

Uncle William, according to Sally, got a job offer to work at a bank in Kansas City as a loan officer back about 1925. He took it and when he left town, his mama cried most of the followin' week. Sally said he done real well up there. He bought some property near town, kept it a couple of years then sold it to the railroad fer a boxcar full of money accordin' to Sally.

He's probably got all the money he ever made 'cause Sally says he's so tight, he squeaks when he walks. I hope it works out fer her.

Ya remember me tellin' ya 'bout that ranch I worked on outside Wheatland, Wyoming? One of the hands there, Casey Russell, guided hunters in the fall mostly for deer and antelope. Doggone if he didn't show up here at the roadhouse with a couple of dudes that came all the way from New York City to hunt Dall Sheep. He was as surprised to see me as I was him. He was quite a sight with a black handlebar moustache, big bushy eyebrows and a faded red bandanna tied around his neck. The black Stetson cocked to the side on his head looked like it had been drug all the way from Wyoming.

I asked him what brought him to Alaska and he said Wyoming was gittin' a little crowded and he decided to come up here to the north country. He said he'd stopped at the roadhouse back a few weeks earlier but there was just an Indian woman runnin' things that day. Said he'd brought in a string of horses he'd wintered over in British Columbia and needed to buy some horseshoes and other supplies.

Now these dudes he brought said they worked at some place called Fifth Avenue back in New York like it was supposed to mean something to me. I told them I didn't care whether they worked on Fifth Avenue or Main Street, they were at Wart's Roadhouse now and it was my rules. The bigger of the two started to get bowed up 'cause of what I said, but Casey got things square with him.

They looked like they was dressed fer their own funeral. Ever thing they had on was brand spankin' new.

Mr. Duncan, the younger of the two, caught me looking at their clothes and gear and promptly told me it was all from Abercrombie and Fitch on Reade Street in New York. I said most of mine came from Taylor Dry Goods back in Anchorage. He said Abercrombie and Fitch were "Outfitters for Sportsmen". I said Taylor Dry Goods sold clothes to real men like miners and trappers. Casey stepped in 'fore it got worse and said he'd buy us all a round of drinks and lets' us sit at the bar.

The two dudes asked to see a wine list but I told 'em I didn't know what they was talking about and I had Tennessee whiskey and rye whiskey. They grumbled somethin' under their breath and finally said they'd drink the Tennessee whiskey. Onced they got some of that down their gullets, they started talking about their fancy gear again. Ya think I cared whether their hats were made by E. A. Mallory and Sons or that their rifles were custom made for them at Abercrombie and Fitch. Mr. Duncan said the rifles were chambered for the .375 H&H Magnum and had stocks of the finest Turkish walnut and had Weaver riflescopes mounted on them. I shouldn't have done it, but I said, "that must be how the two of ya got them nasty cuts over your eyes". That's when Casey jumped up and hustled 'em upstairs to git to bed.

I weren't sad to see 'em go the next morning. They left out on horseback to a spike camp Casey had set up just about a days ride away. That's some pretty country they're headed to, maybe they will appreciate it. Dall sheep hunting is tough on a man's body and mind and I don't believe those dudes got the mind or the body for it.

It's been a long day. I guess I'll finish this up and head off to my bunk.

Wart

SEPTEMBER 1932

'Lo Wart,

Well I've been sitting here at my table in the light of my coal oil lamp putting a box of Peters .22 Shorts in and out of that buckskin bullet pouch Miss Lily made me trying to figure out how I was gonna write you this letter. Well it's jest my nature to tell things straight out and not beat around the bush. So here tis, bout two weeks ago Sally got a telegram from her long lost Kansas uncle's lawyer. Nobody knowed what it said, but according to Sally's sister Maybelle, you know the plump redheaded sister that lives with her, it was disturbing news.

Maybelle told some folks at the store that after Sally got the telegram she went into her bedroom and stayed two days without coming out. It was a mystery to everybody in the valley as to what was going on.

Then two days ago I was picking some green tomatoes out of my garden to pickle fer winter when Sally drove up in that fancy buggie she drives. She got out and shouted in a serious tone to me that she wanted to talk. Well, I got her a glass of buttermilk and we sat on my porch. After talking 'bout the weather and such, she told me she had your rifle in her car and wanted me to keep it fer you. She said she was going on a trip and didn't know how long she would be gone. I jest kept my mouth shut and let her do the talking.

She teared up and wanted to know when I last heard from you. Well, I told her, even told her bout yer new cat. She was glad to hear that. Then she told me she wished things would've been different, that you would've stayed.

Then she swore me to secrecy, but said I could tell you. Her uncle in Kansas died and left her a large sum of money and 28,380 acres in west Kansas near a town called Goodland. To keep the inheritance, she said she has to go to Goodland and live on the property and turn it into a paying cow-calf ranch. That was something her uncle planned to do but spent all his living years making the money and buying land.

I ask her what she was a-gonna do and she told me she was a-gonna move to Goodland the next day, going by train she said. She had her trunk packed and Maybelle was taking her into town so she could catch the train.

After she told me that, she said she didn't want to talk anymore and that she wasn't gonna tell anybody where she was going or how to reach her. She said she loved Tater Knob and the valley but she wanted a fresh start while she was still young enough to do it. We shook hands, I got your rifle and she rode off. I declare, I don't understand women.

Well there you have it, I done told you and I don't know how it's a-gonna strike ye but Sally has her mind made up and she is off to a new life and adventure. In these hard times danged if I ain't plum envious.

On a lighter something, what did you name that cat ye took up with? I would be interested in what a cat does when it needs to go outside and there's three feet of snow.

You was a-telling me 'bout them "know-it-all" dudes that were hunting with that Russell fellow. It was that same type of dude what got Mike Hollinsworth killed over at the Walls. That dude had a gun that were fitten more fer an elephant than a little ol' goat. He was decked out in all new Filson gear and knows more 'bout everything than anybody else.

After we buried Mike, it was all me and the reverend could do to keep some of the boys from going to fetch that dude and bring him back to the gin to hang him. Why is it that during these tough times it seems that it's that sort what has all the money and no sense!

Because the summer were so hot and dry we purt near ain't got no corn or cotton. Shine prices will be at an all time high this winter due to the shortage of corn. Danged, sometimes I wish me and you would've put in a still up at that big hidden spring we found on Hampton Knob, ye remember that spring in the cedar grove that ran a spell and then disappeared under ground. I have thought about that place many times and thought about moving there and just hunt sang, trap and have a hog, cow and a big garden. A fellow could make a go of it up there, but it would be a mighty lonely place. There ain't nobody living within 10 miles of that place. You remember when we stumbled upon it you commented that there ain't a sign that anybody's ever been there.

I went scouting over at Hush Hollow yesterday looking fer a place fer ol' Thunder and me to hunt squirrels in October. Well, that little spring over there is still a-running and that big grove of scaley bark hickories is loaded in nuts. In fact the squirrels are already cutting on them. I plan on getting my squirrel meat there this fall. There are several widow women in the valley hurting fer food due to this hot dry weather so I plan on hunting fer them as well. The good Lord put them bushy tailed tree rats here fer us to eat so I plan on getting enough fer them what's got a near bare cupboard. The reverend said he would help me skin em and deliver em to those what needs em most.

There was big news over at the store yesterday. Jabo Hinson saw a deer come out of his corn field down near the creek. The reverend was with him and he saw it too. Ye know, this is the first deer seen in this neck of the woods since jest after the War Twix the States. The reverend said it left some mighty clear foot prints where it crossed the creek. He was a-wishing fer one of them picture cameras to prove to any doubters that it were a deer.

I wish we had deer like the ol' timers. It would make it easier on many a-families that are struggling to have meat to eat during this depression. If them danged so-called hunters, poachers I say, hadn't of tried to kill every deer they saw, year, round, we would have deer to hunt in the fall and that would be a heap of help during these times. If em goats up in the mountains weren't so dad-blamed hard to get to, they would be gone too. Thank goodness we have them.

Well it was hard to tell you bout Sally, but me and you have always shot straight with one another so I thought I better sit down and let you know what was a-going on. I wish her luck and happiness.

Write back soon and by now you should be enjoying all that hunting fer 'em big critters up there. Sometimes I think I should move there, specially with all this heat and hot weather, but then I think about all that snow. Ye can have it.

Buck

OCTOBER 1932

Hello Buck,

Since yore last letter, I'm settin' here with a heart full of empty. That news 'bout Sally plumb tore me up. I mean I was shocked. I never dreamed her uncle William would do somethin' like that. I knew the old boy was tight but that's a heap of money he made and saved to buy all that land. And still leave Sally a bunch of cash. Whew!

I'm some better now, but when I first read the letter, I felt like I'd been kicked in the gut by that ol'red mule of mine, Dooley. My first thought was to pull the plug on the jug and try to suck the bottom out of it. But I didn't. I did pore me a drink but got to thinkin' that Sally would be real disappointed in me if'n I did somethin' real stupid like get knee walkin' drunk. It were a good thing that Silas was here for the night. He saw I was upset when I grabbed the jug off the back of the bar. I reckon it was when I grabbed a glass and throwed it in the fireplace that he figgered he'd better see what was wrong with me.

Silas is a good sort but I weren't sure I wanted to talk about my feelin's toward Sally's leaving the Knob. I shore wished ya was here to talk it over. The two of us have always been able to talk through the tough times and make sense of things. I felt like one of them volcano's that was 'bout to explode. I ain't never heard Silas speak ill of nobody so I figgered maybe I could talk to him about Sally and he'd understand. I ground up some beans and put on a pot of chicory coffee fer me and Silas. He said it'd be a sight better fer me to drink that coffee than trying to drink the jug dry. He was right.

Fore long the pot was bubblin' and fillin' up the room with a real good smell that made me feel a mite better. Ain't it funny how things like the smell of fresh coffee, grass after a spring rain or a fresh cut watermelon make a fella feel better. Well anyways, I unloaded the whole story to Silas. He listened, nodded his head in understanding ever now and again and told me things he thought would help when he felt like he should. Ya know Buck, I felt a heap better after talkin' to Silas. It weren't the same as talkin' to ya but it did me some good.

I'm real happy that Sally come into good fortune. I understand 'bout her wantin' a fresh start, after all's said and done that's why I left the Knob. Sally did say it right when she said she wished things had been different. I wished I hadn't left the Knob either, now.

I hope she'll be happy and safe and good things will come to her.

There's a real mystery goin' on here at the roadhouse. Ya remember Casey Russell and them two dudes from New York City that went sheep hunting a days ride away. They went over to the other side of Clark mountain to git where Casey's got a base camp set up on the edge of a basin. I been over there huntin' before and that basin must be near 'bout 1000 acres. Anyways, they was supposed to hunt sheep . Cross that basin lies Hope mountain where they was gonna hunt sheep. It's hard country but Casey's a tough hand and growed up hunting and trappin' in the mountains back in Wyoming. I worked with him long enough back in Wyoming to know he can handle most nearly any situation in the backcountry.

They didn't come back to the roadhouse after their hunt and that's what's got me worried. In this country, there's a heap of things that can go wrong. There's avalanches, bears, weather that changes faster than a flea jumps on a hound dog. Ya just don't ever know. I thought maybe I missed 'em when they came through but one of them yankee dudes left his Mackinaw from that fancy store in New York. Wool, red and black plaid and plenty heavy to keep a fella warm. I'd think a fella would pick it on his way out if'n he had come back through headin' home. It does fit me real good though.

There's two more dudes that come to the roadhouse 'bout a week after Casey was supposed to be back. Said he was supposed to be guidin' them for sheep.

They hung around a couple of days then headed back to Talkeetna.

I'm really worried 'bout Casey and his dudes. That area they went to hunt is awful good but the way the land lays with those two mountains comin' together like they do at that basin creates some gosh-awful snow storms even early in the season. I know Casey is tougher than a boiled owl and if there's a fella that can make it out of a calamity, it's Casey.

I ain't told ya that I near 'bout cut off my pointin' finger have I ? I'd gone out caribou huntin' soon after that last letter I sent ya and took me a real good one in an area just west of here. I was up to my elbows dressin' out that rascal and was tryin' to cut through it's windpipe when my knife closed on my finger. I pulled my hand out of that caribou and lifted the knife blade off my finger and the blood left a neat half moon shape on the blade. I tore off a piece of my shirt fer a bandage, wrapped my finger, and went back to cleanin' the big critter except with my belt knife.

After I got back to the roadhouse and got the meat put up, Lily Johns saw the finger and asked what happened. I told her then she wanted to take a look at my finger. She decided my finger needed to be sewed up with a couple of stitches. I hate to say it but she was right cause the cut was splayed open and oozin'. She got one of her sewing needles and got me fixed up right good.

A few day's later, I was workin' in the blacksmith shop and saw me a little piece of steel 'bout 6 inches long and got me an idea. I made me a little fixed blade knife that sure won't close on my finger. I found me some latigo leather in the back of the shop and made me a little pouch sheath fer it. It'll fit in my pocket, on my belt or I can put a rawhide thong through the loop and wear it around my neck where it's real handy. I'll make ya up one if you like.

I'm real glad Jabo and the preacher saw them deer tracks back at the Knob. I hope they'' take up there again. They eat real good. I eat a bunch of deer meat on my travels at the different places I worked. Out west, they got what they call a mule deer cause it's got bigger ears than a regular deer. There's a bunch of 'em too. I taught the boys at the Bar N ranch how to make jerky with it. They didn't know how. Hard to believe a fella workin' on a ranch don't how to make jerky. There's been many a day you and me woulda been hungry if it hadn't been fer some jerky.

Buck, I've been thinkin' a lot 'bout things lately. I was wonderin' if I came back to the Knob fer a visit, could I stay with ya? Have ya still got that ol' rope bed in the back room? There's a feelin' in my bones that's leadin' me to come home fer a spell. I can't rightly explain it. I'd like to see all the folks back there, go squirrel huntin' with ya and Ol' Thunder over at Hush Hollow and be there with ever body at Christmas. I don't know how long I'll stay but I promise I won't be a burden to ya.

Silas had been talkin' some 'bout how hard the travelin's been on him this fall, what with that broke arm he got when he fell off the roof of his cabin. Seems he was trying to patch the roof last month fore the bad weather set in fer good, lost his balance and fell onto the woodpile and broke his right arm. I asked him if he'd like to stay here and run the roadhouse if I went back home fer a spell and he 'bout fell outta his chair tellin' me how good he'd take care of things and not to worry.

If'n ya say it's ok to stay with ya, I'll start headin' back now that I know Silas can handle things up here. Onced, I get to Seattle, I'll catch a train and head home. I will tell ya that I'm gonna stop in Goodland, Kansas and check on Sally to see if she's doin' well and if I can help her in any way. When the train gits to Memphis, I'll send ya a telegram from the station so ya'll know when to expect me. I expect it to be the third week of December.

Lordy, it'll shore be good to be back at the Knob.

Buck

NOVEMBER 1932

'Lo Wart,

That is exciting news about you coming home fer a long visit. There's a heap of folks here that will be glad to see you. I will clean up that back room fer you and check it fer fleas. Ol' Thunder stays there some but he don't like the corn shuck mattress so he sleeps on that ol' spotted steer hide I have on the floor.

Maybelle jest got a post from Sally and she has taken a shine to being a rancher. She wrote Maybelle that she has bought herself a fine black mare and a hand tooled Mexican style saddle and is getting to know the country she inherited. She is now all bronzed from being out in the sun and is spending her days buying cattle, hiring hands to mend and build fences and building a ranch headquarters. Who would've ever thought that purty little woman would become a cattle baroness? Fer sure not me. I think if you stop there on yore way home you are going to be in fer a big surprise. Tell her I said howdy and that the whole valley misses her sweet smile.

I'm plum sorry you cut yore pointing finger but it was good that that miss Lily knew how to sew. I learned the hard way that a cut made on yore hide while cleaning game can fester up and get bad fast. I cut the palm of my left hand two years ago while skinning rats and didn't soak it in coal oil or sew it up and it danged near rotted off. When I went to see Doc bout it, he screamed at me and made a big fuss bout dying and such. It took two months fer it to get back right. Now I've got a quarter moon scar to remind me not to do that again. A gypsy fortune reader set up a tent near the gin a couple of months ago and read peoples palm fer a quarter a read. Well I traded her wooden spoon I carved from cedar fer a reading. When I opened up my palm with that scar in it she jumped up looking big-eyed and scared and said she could find no fortune signs in that pile of skin. She said that it looked like the devil might be in me. The next morning her tent and she was gone. Some said I run her off, some was glad, they's didn't want no gypsy's in the valley.

You mentioned making a fixed-blade knife, bring it home with you when you come. I been a-wanting one but I was in Montgomery Ward a few weeks back and they's wanted $2.00 fer one. I can't afford that, but we could get out in the barn and make one if'en you bring yours fer us to go by. I've been a-wanting a fixed-blade knife fer a long time and it will really come in handy when hunting them billy goats way back in the mountains and jest doing camp chores and such.

I hope that Russell fellow and his dudes make it back to your roadhouse fore you leave. You seem to like that fellow and you don't need to have that hunting party's fate hanging up in yore mind while you be here. They's probably hung up in a camp somewhere snowed in. If'n Russell is as good as you think he is, he can handle it with no problem. He might have his hand full sitting on em city fellows as they can be a might fidgety when sitting out bad weather.

One year I took three city fellows down to Hobbs Island in the Tennessee River on a duck hunt. I was to take em to the island in my boat, build camp, cook and help em clean ducks they kilt. Well the second day they was a-hunting a heavy fog came in and sit right down on the river. I had to go find those dudes and bring em back to camp.

Fer three days that fog sat on us, I couldn't hardly see good enough to cook vittles fer em, much less pack up and go. Well, em fellows almost started a fight with me to try to pack up and hit the river to go home. We'd all drown in that cold water if'n we'd tried it. I had to be downright stern with em. So I know what that Russell fellow is going through. If all else fails ye got yeself a good coat out of the deal, he, he.

Jabo has been looking fer that deer ever since he and the reverend saw him, but that deer was jest passing through. I think it will be a long spell fore we can quit eating goat and have deer to eat. I see them deer pictures in them sporting magazines and I shore would like to hunt me one.

Ol' Thunder and I have been wearing em squirrels out over in Hush Hollow. It's a long ways over there but lordy there is a lot of squirrels in those big hickories. With crops dried up, I got a lot of time to hunt this year. On one of our hunts over there Ol' Thunder treed in a big hollow beech tree and I had to build a little fire in the ground level opening in the tree to see what was in it. I put me on some green leaves on that little fire and got a good smoke a-going. Well, out popped a big coon at the top of the hollow tree trunk, I shot him, then another, then another.

I had three 15 pound coons and four squirrels when I decided to walk back home. It was a job to tote all that game back to my house. But it was worth it as Mrs. Maude Cooper was down with the flu and fresh coon made her smile real big. Her husband, bless his soul, he can't hardly walk due to rheumatism, told the reverend he believes they would have starved to death had I not brought 'em that meat. It's good the Lord provides fer 'em what ain't got much during these trying times.

Well, it's time to get my traplines set out. By the time you get here I will have 'em working and you can run the lines with me jest like the good ol' days. With that Silas fellow running the roadhouse you can stay a spell here at the Knob. We jest might go up to that hidden spring up on Hampton Knob and talk 'bout the possibilities of it being a base camp fer huntin' sang and trapping. Heck, with some clearing a fellow might could grow a crop up on that flat top.

I'll be looking forward to getting yore telegram when you gets to Memphis mid month. Let me know which train station ye'll be coming to and I will meet you there. The whole valley will be anxious to hear yore stories 'bout that cold north country. The reverend said this will be a grand Christmas at the church having you back and that bunch what sits around the stove at the store can't wait to spin yarns with ye. You have become somewhat of a legend here 'bouts.

Travel safe and don't ferget to bring that knife you made.

Buck

P.S.: I shore would be nice if you could get some Kodak pictures of the roadhouse, Lily and Silas. I'd like to see one of yore cache. Jest thought I would ask.

END

Appendix

This book was first released as an e-book and has generated so many requests for copies of the recipes of country dishes mentioned in the book that the authors decided to write them in the same format and put them in this paper book as an appendix.

We hope you enjoy them as much as the authors have.

Divide Camp Biscuits

It's been a spell since I heard from you. I guess with winter coming on and such up there in Alaska you have a lot to do to get ready fer the long darkness.

The last time you wrote you was a-wishing fer some of those biscuits I use to cook fer us when we was a-living over the Divide in that old logging camp and digging sang.

Well, I finally got all my traps ready fer the coming trapping season and got in my little crop of cotton so sat down and put pen to paper and wrote up the recipe with some of yer other favorites. Here 'tis.

1 cup flour

1 1/2 teaspoon baking powder

1 1/2 teaspoon sugar

1/8 teaspoon salt

1/4 cup butter

1/3 cup milk or buttermilk

1. Stir together flour, baking powder, sugar and salt.

2. Cut in butter until mixture resembles coarse crumbs.

3. Make a well and in the middle of the mixture and stir in milk.

4. Knead on floured surface a few times. Work dough as little as possible.

5. Roll dough to 1/2 inch thickness. Cut with a 2 inch cutter.

6. Transfer to aluminum pan in Dutch oven

7. Bake at 450o for 10–12 minutes. Makes 7 biscuits.

Sawmill Gravy Recipe

"Now you know, Wart, that a biscuit without sawmill gravy is jest a nekkid biscuit so I thought I'd better include my momma's sawmill gravy recipe jest so you'd have it. I think you already know it but it was named "sawmill gravy" back in the 1800's when the cook's at remote sawmill sites had to feed a lot of hard working, hungry men. The budget for food was limited so the cook substituted biscuits and flour gravy for meat. The gravy became known as "sawmill gravy" and it kept a lot of us fed while working trap lines. Here's how I make it these days."

3 tablespoons of bacon, sausage, squirrel, groundhog or pork chop

drippings, if'n you got meat.

1/4 cup all purpose flour

1/2 teaspoon salt

1/2 teaspoon black pepper

1 1/2 cups milk

1. Pour the meat drippings into a medium skillet over medium heat.

2. Add flour and stir to combine. Add salt and pepper.

3. Cook and stir until flour begins to brown.

4. Slowly pour in the milk while stirring constantly to break up any lumps.

5. Lower heat to low and continue cooking and stirring until gravy thickens.

6. For thinner gravy add milk.

7. Serve hot over biscuits, pork chops, mashed taters or skillet fried steak.

Skillet Fried Steak

"Now's that I brung up skillet fried steak I'm a-betting you don't remember how we cooked up those beef and venison cubed steaks we loved so much when we was living on the trap line up near the Walls. You remember it tasted best when cooked in that old cast iron skillet that the widow Sally Jensen gave you fer Christmas that winter.

Dang, it makes my mouth jest a-watering to think about those skillet fried steaks with a big dob of sawmill gravy on it. Be sure to write this one down and the next time you come back to Tater Knob I will give you that cast iron skillet. I have it hanging on the wall inside the smokehouse.

To make the steaks, gather up these fixings and git started."

- 2 pieces cubed steak

- 1 cup all-purpose flour

- 1/2 tsp salt

- 1/2 teaspoon black pepper

- Vegetable oil for frying

1. Pour oil to a depth of 1/4 inch in a large cast iron skillet. Place over medium heat while you prepare the cubed steaks.

2. In a bowl, stir together flour, salt, and pepper. In another bowl, pour milk.

3. Dip each piece of meat into milk on both sides, then flour mixture on

both sides, back in milk on both sides, and back in flour mixture on both sides.

Repeat until both pieces of meat are breaded.

4. Carefully place in hot oil and cook until browned on both sides, about 8-10 minutes. Remove to paper towel lined plate while you prepare the sawmill gravy.

5. Pour sawmill gravy over steaks and enjoy.

Fort Concho Peach Cobbler

"Writing all this made me to go to thinking about a good desert recipe that we use to like when we spent that summer running trotlines on the Tennessee River with that old one-eyed cowboy who lived in that shack near Painted Bluff.

You might remember he had that peach orchard behind his place and he use to cook what he called his Fort Concho Peach Cobbler and lordy that was some kind of good cobbler. I got him to write the recipe down and ever now and then when I come on some fresh peaches I fix me one of them cobblers. Here is a copy fer you."

Cobbler crust

2 cups flour

1/2 teaspoon salt

1 teaspoon baking powder

1 teaspoon sugar

6 tablespoons shorting

1/4 cup water

1. Mix dry ingredients, add shorting and cut in with two knives. Mixture should resemble course corn meal.

2. Add cold water gradually to make a ball.

3. Divide into two balls for top and bottom 9-inch cobbler crust.

4. Roll out on floured surface with rolling pin.

5. Place one crust in bottom of pan, add filling.

6. Top with remaining crust or strips of crust in latticework pattern.

Filler

1 cup sugar

6 cups fresh peaches, peeled and sliced

1 cup butter

1 cup brown sugar

1 teaspoon cinnamon

1/2 cup Jack Daniel's whiskey

1 1/2 cups whipping cream

1. Preheat 12-inch Dutch oven to 350 degrees

2. Melt butter in saucepan.

3. Add peaches, brown sugar, cinnamon, sugar, and cream.

4. Bring to a boil and simmer for 10 minutes. Add whiskey and stir easily.

5. Cook for 15 minutes.

6. Line a 9-inch aluminum pan with cobbler crust.

7. Pour in peach filler.

8. Cover top with whole crust or strips of crust.

9. Bake for 45 to 50 minutes.

Enough fer 8 regular people or three river rats.

Mrs. Martin's Hearty Grits

"We ain't mentioned grits and I know you must be a-starving fer a big plate of grits to go with 'em biscuits. The recipe that I'm using these days I got from Reverend Martin's wife. You remember those breakfast's she use to cook when we helped dig a grave at the church cemertary.

Her grits were the best I ever ate. She was a bit stubborn 'bout letting me have this here recipe so keep it under your hat. Here tis."

4 cups water

1 cup natural grits

3 Tbsp. chicken broth

2 tbsp. minced garlic

2 tbsp. butter

1 cup shredded sharp cheddar cheese

1/2 cup Half & Half

Salt/pepper to taste, use Smokehouse Black Pepper

1. Bring water, garlic, broth and butter to a boil in heavy sauce pan.

2. Add grits and reduce heat to low.

3. Cook for 20 minutes or until grits are soft. Stir often

4. Add cheese and Half & Half. Stir until cheese melts.

5. Serve hot, goes good with hoe cake.

WART'S SODA BREAD

"It's only right for me to send a few of the recipes the trappers, hunters, hermits and other ne'er-do-wells really like for me to fix here at the roadhouse since ya shared recipes with me. I know

I've told you about the trapper 3-finger Jack Driscoll. He's one of the regulars what comes in for supplies and to drop off furs for the fur buyer. He really likes my soda bread and always buys himself a loaf to take back to his cabin. My great grandmother (on the McGee side) passed this recipe down to my mama years ago and mama taught me how to make it.

You'll probably remember mama making it for us before we'd take off for several days running our trap lines up near the Tennessee line. Here is how she makes it:"

1 1/2 cups buttermilk

3 cups flour

1/2 cup sugar

1 tbsp baking powder

1/2 teaspoon soda

1/2 tsp salt

1 cup raisins

Mix the ingredients, except the buttermilk, in a bowl. Add the buttermilk slowly and stir until the milk is absorbed. Dump on a floured board and knead thoroughly. If sticky, add more flour. Form an oval with the dough and cut across the top of the dough in a shallow X. Place in your Dutch oven, wood stove or reflector oven and cook 'til ready, usually about 45 minutes.

BAR-N STEW

"I tell you Buck, of all the places I worked during my travels, I reckon I enjoyed working on the Bar-N ranch in southeast Wyoming probably the most.

Actually, the time I spent breaking horses I didn't enjoy at all but it was part of the job. We'd go up into the high country to hunt mule deer and there was times I'd be sitting in the rimrock looking for game and it seemed like I could see forever.

Sam Neely, the owner of the ranch, is an easy-going rancher who growed up in the ranching business. He said his mama schooled him at home but when he turned 13, he pretty much went to cowboying full time with his daddy and never looked back. He told me it was in his blood and couldn't imagine doing nothing else. He sure taught me a bunch about cattle and horses and

I thought I knew a right smart about 'em having growed up around them on the home place at Tater Knob.

Back home, we can grow a cow and calf on an acre of pasture but out here, it takes about 100 acres for a cow and calf for 'em to get by. His ranch is pretty near 10,000 acres and it takes a lot of time horseback to work the herd, particularly in calving season. It's shore 'nuff big country!

Missus Neely kept her family and us ranch hands fed real good. She made this stew a good bit and there was rarely any left over. When I asked her what she called it, she shrugged her shoulders and said it didn't have a name but she guessed she would call it Bar-N stew."

5-6 pieces of thick sliced bacon cut into 1 inch pieces

2 pounds stew meat (beef, venison, antelope, elk) cut into 1 inch cubes

4 large potatoes, peeled and cut into bite size cubes

6 carrots, peeled and cut into 1 inch pieces

1 large onion peeled and diced

1 cabbage cored and coarsely chopped

1 can whole kernel corn

Salt and pepper to taste

Cook the bacon in the Dutch oven until crisp, remove and set aside

Put the meat in the pan and cook until browned

Add water to the pan to cover the meat by 1 inch

Bring to a boil, and then simmer about 1 1/2 hours with the lid on the pot

Add the potatoes, onion and carrots and simmer 30 minutes more

Stir in the cabbage and corn and cook until the vegetables are tender

Serve with a skillet of hot cornbread and butter.

Aunt Willie's Baked Rabbit (Tundra Baked Rabbit)

"After I got up here to Alaska and took over the roadhouse, I was really surprised to learn there's rabbits up here and they're right plentiful most years. Well, they're not really rabbits but they're called artic hares and larger than the cottontails we like to hunt back home. I don't think they're any bigger than the canecutter rabbits we like to hunt in the bottoms over near the Flint River. You can hunt 'em anytime of the year but fall seems to be the best season to do it.

I cook 'em like my Aunt Willie showed me back home. Mama never would cook 'em for me and daddy cause she said they reminded her of the little white Easter bunny she got when she was 6 or 7. She didn't mind me and daddy hunting them with Tober and Little Red, but she wasn't gonna cook rabbits, now that's for sure. So me and daddy would go over to Aunt Willies and she would cook 'em and we'd eat with her that night.

I know you still haven't forgotten that time we were hunting rabbits with AW Gardner at his place and Tober and Little Red started running that big canecutter that we kicked up on the backside of his farm. The dogs stayed gone so long, we thought they'd gotten lost but after about 45 minutes, here they come back running that big canecutter and all 3 of 'em had their tongues hanging out and were looking for relief. The rabbit got his. The dogs were so tired, they looked like they wanted to meet the same fate that rabbit did.

Aunt Willie taught me several different ways to cook rabbit but I think this recipe is my favorite. The regulars here at the roadhouse seem to like it real well and they call it "tundra rabbit."

1 rabbit, cut up into pieces

1/3 cup lard or oil

2 cups hot water

4 cups cut up vegetables, carrots, potatoes, onions, peas (whatever you got handy)

1 teaspoon salt

1/4 cup flour

Salt, pepper and additional flour

Roll the rabbit pieces in a mixture of salt, pepper and flour

Heat the lard or oil and slowly brown the rabbit turning it often. Drain lard or oil from skillet

Add hot water and put the cover on your iron skillet

Bake the rabbit at medium temperature (325-350) for 1 1/2 hours

Add vegetables and cook 30 minutes more

Mix the 1/4 cup flour with a little cold water and several tablespoons of liquid from the skillet and stir into the liquid in the pan

Cook until the gravy is smooth and thick

AUNT EFFIE'S RAISIN PIE

"Mama (mostly) and Aunt Willie taught me a lot about cooking and I'm sure glad they did cause it comes in real handy for single fella to be able to cook himself some good meals when he's a mind to. For sure, it comes in real handy running this roadhouse.

Heck, ever body that eats here says it's a heap better eatin' here than before I took the place over and that makes me right proud. Most of these ol' sourdoughs seem to live off jerky, hardtack and pemmican, maybe that's why they seem so out of sorts when they show up here at the roadhouse. They always eat like they're starvin' when they get here to the roadhouse, it don't seem to matter what's on the menu that day. Another thing, they gobble desserts down like a kid in a candy store.

I've learned to always make more desserts than I think I will need.I always thought mama made the best peach and apple pies around but she never made a raisin pie.

Well, about 7 or 8 years ago, Piney Grove Church had a revival with dinner on the grounds and the old maid school teacher Miss Effie Pratt brought 2 raisin pies for the meal. I really didn't want to try any but since she had been my favorite teacher, I took a piece to please her. Dadgum, if I didn't like it and went back for more!

I told mama about it and she got the recipe from Miss Effie and would make 'em at home from time to time. She taught me how to make 'em and I make 'em fairly regularly here at Wart's Roadhouse. Remember that trapper named Shamus O'Kelly from over near Porkypine Creek I've told you about, he's eaten a whole raisin pie at one sitting but then he is a big, burly red-headed devil with an appetite to match. Ol' Silas Wooten the drummer that keeps me in supplies for the roadhouse, says raisins are almost as hard to find in Alaska as grits.

He does a good job, though, of keepin' me supplied with raisins cause he has surely fallen in love with those pies."

1 1/2 cup raisins

1 1/2 cup water

1 1/2 cup brown sugar

2 tbsp. butter (Miss Effie told mama to use fresh churned butter if she could)

Put the above in the pot and cook for 5 minutes

Add the following:

2 egg yolks beaten

1 tsp. lemon juice

3 tbsp. dissolved in 3 tbsp. of water

Cook for 5 minutes stirring constantly then remove from stove and let cool slightly

Pour into a baked pie crust and allow to cool 40-45 minutes

Top it with whipped cream or meringue

Well Buck, it's late and I'm wore down to a knob about like this pencil I'm using, so I guess I'll close this letter.

Always good to hear from you and news from back home.

Tell ever body ol' Warts sends his regards.

Wart

About the Authors

J. Wayne Fears

J. Wayne Fears has been an outdoor writer for over four decades. During that period of time he has written for most of the major outdoor magazines. He has authored over 6,000 outdoor magazine articles and 32 books on a variety of outdoor subjects including hunting, fishing, canoeing, cooking, wildlife management and backcountry survival. He has also written fiction and humor. He has received numerous awards for his writing and conservation work. He was voted into the Explorers Club and in 2012 he was enshrined into the Legends of the Outdoors Hall of Fame. To learn more about him and his other writings go to www.jwaynefears.com

J. Craig Haney

J. Craig Haney grew up in town but his heart and DNA were in the outdoors. Growing up, he spent as much time as possible in the rural areas and backcountry of North Alabama where he learned numerous outdoor skills from relatives, scalawags, and other ne'er do wells. Over the years, he has worked as a manufacturers rep of outdoor products, fly shop operator, lake and stream fishing guide and taught a variety of topics on deer hunting, turkey hunting, survival, cooking and outdoor skills. His articles and pictures have appeared in a number of national and regional publications. ***Backcountry Letters of Buck and Wart***, co-written with J.Wayne Fears, is his first book.

To learn more about him and his other writings go to www.jcraighaney.com.

Other Books by J. Wayne Fears

Isaac – Trek to King's Mountain
Chipmunk, Punky, Sometimes Jenny, and Me
Deer Hunters Reference Guide
How to Manage Native Plants for Deer
How to Hunt Clear Cuts
How to Make Jerky & Pemmican
How to Lost-Proof Your Child
The Complete Book of Dutch Oven Cooking
The Pocket Survival Guide
Hunt Club Management Guide
Hunting Whitetails East & West
Build Your Dream Cabin in the Woods
The Complete Book of Outdoor Survival
The Field & Stream Wilderness Cooking Handbook
The Canoer's Bible
Hunting Big Bears – Brown, Grizzly and Polar Bears
Hunting Whitetails Successfully
Muzzleloading Hunters Handbook
Cooking the Wild Harvest
The Wild Turkey Book
Successful Turkey Hunting
The Complete Book to Canoe Camping
Sportsman's Guide to Swamp Camping
Trout Fishing the Southern Appalachians
Turkey Guide
Planting for Wildlife
Hunting North America's Big Bear
Scrape Hunting from A to Z
Backcountry Cooking

If you enjoyed "Buck & Wart – Backcountry Letters," then you'll love:

Chipmunk, Punky, Sometimes Jenny and Me

For several years well known outdoor writer J. Wayne Fears has written his comic tall tales about growing up poor around Tater Knob Mountain. They have been hits in magazines such as *Progressive Farmer*, *GunHunter* and *Great Days Outdoors*. Now he has compiled many of the folksy tales, which have the humor similar to Pat McManus with the rural nostalgic, philosophical touch similar to Ferrol Sams, into a book entitled *Chipmunk, Punky, Sometimes Jenny and Me*.

These short stories takes you on boyhood adventures and misadventures including hunting trophy green hole possums, fishing for hornyheads, defeating ginseng thieves, attending flea infested weddings, trapping black panther's and disturbing Maude

Culpepper's ghost. You will get to know Fears boyhood buddies Chipmunk, Punky, Jenny, Snake, Dutch, Ball Ping and many more as they search for ways to become rich and famous in the outdoors.

Each tale in this collection of short stories will keep the young adult and adult reader coming back for more. *Chipmunk, Punky, Sometimes Jenny and Me* transports the reader to a more simple place and time, and keeps him laughing all the way.

http://www.amazon.com/dp/B009ED26R4.

The Briar Patch Philosopher

"The Briar Patch Philosopher" by John e. Phillips, is a collection of wise sayings that are simple to remember. One of my favorites that I learned from my dad was, "Even the good will of a bad dog is worth something." We all face bad dogs in our work places, in our families and with our friends. By getting the good will of bad dogs on your side, you make the dog's biting you very difficult

In the briar patch of life, you'll encounter thorns, hurts, disappointments, various trials, danger and missteps all along the way.

Also, in the briar patch of life, you'll find the true virtues that are necessary - courage, endurance, patience, faith and wisdom. If you're willing to run through the briar patch and the fires of everyday living, and you rely heavily on courage, endurance, patience, faith and wisdom, you can have a happy, successful, prosperous and meaningful life.

http://www.amazon.com/Briar-Patch-Philosopher-John-Phillips-ebook

Isaac – Trek to King's Mountain

Isaac was 14 years old happy boy living on a small remote wilderness farm when his father was killed by the British in 1780 during the Revolutionary War.

The men in the overmountain farms and settlements quickly formed an army, unpaid, untrained, with little organization or leadership and began the historic trek over the Appalachian Mountains in search of Ferguson and his Loyalists troops to defeat him. Isaac, against his mother's will joined the rag-tag army and begin the historic trek to find the British.

Based on a true story, you will go with Isaac, Reuben McGee, his dog Rufus on the well over 100 mile trek during which they dealt with possible Indian attacks, not knowing where the British were, horrible weather, traitors and an always shortage of food and supplies.

It is a compelling adventure story about men going up against all odds, and coming out victorious. Isaac – Trek to King's Mountain is well known outdoor book author, J. Wayne Fears, at his best!

http://www.amazon.com/Isaac-Kings-Mountain-Wayne-Fears-ebook/dp/B008JOIRSG

Made in United States
Orlando, FL
02 May 2022